In Mrs. Tully's Room

In Mrs. Tully's Room

Room

A Childcare Portrait

VIVIAN GUSSIN PALEY

HARVARD UNIVERSITY PRESS

Cambridge, Massachusetts, and London, England 2001

Library of Congress Cataloging-in-Publication Data

Paley, Vivian Gussin, 1929–
  In Mrs. Tully's room : a childcare portrait / Vivian Gussin Paley.
    p. cm.
  ISBN 0-674-00632-1
   1. Tully, Lillian.   2. Day care centers—Illinois—Chicago.   3. Child
care workers—Illinois—Chicago.   4. Education, Preschool—Illinois—
Chicago.   5. Storytelling.   6. Storytelling ability in children.   I. Title.

HQ778.67.C55 P35 2001
372.21—dc21   2001016966

To our grandchildren
Danny, Michelle, and Debbie

We know by experience itself that it is a marvelous pain to find out but a short way by long wandering.

—Roger Ascham, The Schoolmaster (1570)

In this, the fifth year of my retirement from the classroom, I am an easy mark for almost any hospitable gesture. A tall, dark, smiling woman hands me a book to sign, then issues an invitation I cannot refuse. "Would you care to see the truly youngest storytellers? The twos?"

Her name tag reads "Lillian Tully, Chicago, Illinois" but her voice says New Orleans. This is where I first began to teach, though not children as young as two. "That's a tempting offer," I reply. "I don't know the twos."

"Well, one thing, they keep their stories short," she laughs, printing her name, address, and phone number for me. "And we act the stories out too, sort of the way you do it. At least I think we do. But it seems too easy. Maybe you might tell me if I'm missing something?"

It does seem too easy. For a number of years I've been walking into classrooms asking young children to tell me their stories so we may act them out. They do not know me but are eager to do me this favor, as if they have only been waiting to be asked. How nice to meet another teacher who also wonders why it is so easy.

The following week I am in a childcare center in an old part of town. A small sign on the office door reads "Lillian Tully, director and head teacher." I am shown to a chair and immediately there are eight two-year-olds speeding around me, each going in a different direction. Later I'll visit the threes, fours, and fives whom I can easily imagine slowing down to tell a story, but these twos seem more interested in darting from one activity to another in the shortest period of time.

Big soft pillows on the floor cushion their tumbles and adult laps offer further comfort, but the stop and go rhythm is unlike anything I am used to in a classroom. This is uncharted territory for me. Surely the children are too young to be away from home, yet they seem to own everything they touch. "Mine!"

they announce and then move on. It is a doll corner in motion and the children themselves are the dolls, carrying supplies in buggies and baskets to every other corner of the room. Mrs. Tully and her colleagues, Connie and Maureen, greet the children each time they pass, by name and destination, establishing the purposefulness of their comings and goings.

A boy named Alex comes to a halt at Mrs. Tully's chair. "Mama," he says, and his teacher prints "MAMA" on unlined paper. She waits for more, pen in midair. "Mama you say?"

"Mama," he repeats, and is gone before further information can be solicited. "Mama" is the first story of the day. It will be acted out with several others dictated during the next thirty minutes. Along with everything else going on, the twos are doing stories. "Doing" is the verb of choice.

Valerie, a serious girl with ribboned braids, comes out of the doll corner wearing a pink quilted bed jacket and escorts me to the rug. "We doing stories," she tells me, solemnly eyeing the papers on Mrs. Tully's lap.

Perhaps Valerie wonders if her words are still intact. A three-year-old in my class once seemed offended, after a second or third hearing of *The Carrot Seed,* that the little boy's family was still telling him his carrot wouldn't come up. "They did that the other time," she protested.

The constancy of the printed page may be in doubt, but the twos have learned a few other things about the storytelling practiced in Mrs. Tully's room. To begin with, they know whom the words come from and what they are meant to convey.

"We'll do Alex now," Mrs. Tully decides, holding up his paper. He moves to the center of the rug and stands motionless, arms folded across his striped shirt. "Mama," she reads, stretching the word into a sentence.

"Do it again," tiny Angela whispers. Mrs. Tully nods, then pronounces "Mama" even more slowly, as if she and the children have begun a waltz. Alex beams at Angela and raises both arms above his head.

"My turn! Me!" she calls and he pulls her onto the rug. The teacher narrates the one-word epic a third time, then a fourth and a fifth, until all eight children have come forward. Each acts the role according to some inner logic: this one walks on his toes, another bends to touch the rug, someone else closes her eyes and sways. With every new interpretation the suspense builds. Simone, the last, says, "Look at me, Alex. I'm Mama."

Mrs. Tully's words come back to me. "Maybe you might tell me if I'm missing something." Instead I think of what she has gained, seeing the drama unfold in the company of two-year-olds. Their ability to bring a character to life and reveal something about themselves at the same time is astonishing. They are *doing* stories. Doing goes beyond pretending and telling; doing is the final process, or at least the sum of events up to a particular moment.

Mrs. Tully does not rush through these experiences; nor did I when I had my own classroom. I too learned to slow down and allow each scene to play itself out. Midway into my teaching career, in fact, I extended my kindergarten to a full-day program in order to have more time for stories. It marked the beginning of a new way of teaching for me, a reconstitution of what was meant to happen each day in the classroom.

"We'll do Sidney," Mrs. Tully says. His is a three-word story, which now seems long to me. "Mommy wipe up," she reads. I notice that his story paper is scribbled all over, perhaps intended to represent the wiping motions.

"Is that the table she's wiping up?" Mrs. Tully asks.

"Is dishes and 'poons," Sidney answers. As if by magic, each child is transformed into a curved object while the author runs about wiping arms and heads. The choreography for Valerie's story is no less explicit. "Tuck me in baby" is her script and she glides in between seven curled-up babies, pulling up imaginary blankets. "Sleepy, sleepy," she murmurs to Alex, gently lowering his head.

The twos reach the essence of a scene with the speed of a sprinter. Whatever the message they act out, it comes across as "You are my friend because I am in your story." On the playground, I tell Mrs. Tully how much I admire the way she does stories. "It's such a total group experience with the twos, almost the opposite of the way they handle everything else. By the way, are their stories always about mothers?"

"Mostly, yes," she says. "Seems like the best reason to tell a story, when you are two, is to keep Mama in mind. And to get everyone to do something with you on your terms. Maybe you're not so lonely then."

She jumps up to catch Angela at the bottom of the slide and I stare after her, wondering who Lillian Tully is, this profound thinker in the realm of the truly youngest storytellers. I do not want to leave this place where stories are being explained to me in new ways. Keeping Mama in mind is something I've taken for granted, yet suddenly it seems a crucial impetus, a prime factor in making a child this young want to slow down and tell a story.

"Still and all, who knows what else is going on," Mrs. Tully says, returning to the bench. "It's a mystery, don't you think? I mean, the way these babies take to storytelling it's like they were born doing it. Funny thing, most folks I meet at conferences don't even know the twos can do it. Even though it's nothing different than play."

For some children, however, even play is a mystery. "There was a boy named Paul," I tell Mrs. Tully, "a young three, in my nursery school class. He refused to leave my side the first two weeks of school, held my hand, sat on my lap, or just plain leaned against me, wherever I was. Then one day, sitting next to me on the playground, he asked me, 'Why are all these kids here?' He'd been trying to figure that out. Apparently, the adult explanations made no sense and even the children's play was confusing."

Sidney has brought a pail of sand and dumped it next to Mrs. Tully's feet. Then he begins to spoon it back into the pail, listening to the adult conversation.

"Finally, the beginning of the third week, a boy he'd been watching dictated a story. Paul was on my lap while I wrote it down and still there when we acted it out. But when the boy walked into the middle of the rug, Paul got down and followed him. From then on, Paul began to play, cautiously and at first only with this boy, but the crisis was over."

"What was the story?" Mrs. Tully asks, brushing sand from Sidney's hair.

"One word, an Alex-type story. Only this was the boy's name, Fredrick. But something cleared up for Paul. Maybe 'Fredrick' is just another version of the Mama story."

"You mean like, I'm still the same person I was at home with Mama? Or maybe even, *this* is who I am. Step one, look at me. Step two, pretend you're me?"

"Step three," Sidney murmurs to himself, poking his teacher's shoe with a spoonful of sand. His use of a teaspoon to shovel the sand back into his pail ensures him slow but steady progress and keeps him within touching distance of Mrs. Tully a while longer.

I feel the same way. I want to offer her little spoonfuls of anecdotes so we can chat back and forth while watching the children play. All these maybes and what ifs and wonder whys fill my soul with pleasures I've not feasted on since leaving my classroom. Soon Mrs. Tully will add a great deal more for me to contemplate, her own stories, and they do not stray far from Mama, as I am about to discover.

She usually has her snack time with the twos. "The olders are a bit more patient," she says. "If I don't get around to them before lunch, they don't worry that I'm not coming. So, generally, I'm with the twos until their naps."

It is clear that the children are waiting for a story. "When I was a little girl with ribbons on my head," Mrs. Tully begins, "Mama let us feed the chicks."

Maria sings out, "Lalalana!"

"That's right, baby, in Louisiana." The children know this place where their teacher was a little girl with ribbons on her head. "And we had a cow named Miranda. Did I tell you about her? She gave us such good sweet milk, sweet as . . ."

"Honeysucker onabine," Valerie finishes the sentence and Mrs. Tully repeats, "Sweet as honeysuckle on the vine. That's just how sweet Miranda's milk was."

Suddenly I want to tell everyone how the honeysuckle in our New Orleans garden climbed all over the dogwood tree and my own little boys called it "Jack and the Beanstalk." I never told my kindergartners about this and now I wonder why. In any case, it is Mrs. Tully's "honeysucker onabine," not mine, in this classroom.

She waits for the juice cups to be drained. "Here's how we fed our baby chicks. Make your hands into a cup like this, then let Mama pour in the yellow corn like so. Then you say, 'Chick-a-chick, come pick-a-pick' and all those baby chicks come running. When Miranda sees them, she laughs her moo-ha-ha laugh."

The little ones echo their teacher's sound effects while she pours out more feed for her barnyard chorus. Every child is now tossing imaginary yellow corn into the air and watching it float to the ground. The ease with which a simple story can mobilize a group of children is well known, but the mood of these two-year-olds goes beyond a playful call and response. They follow Mrs. Tully inside her Mama story as effortlessly as they did Alex in his, though she pictures a scene they could not have experienced.

"Where your mama at?" Alex wants to know, grabbing his teacher's little finger.

"Where's my mama at? Probably at home cooking stew, with carrots and beans and cabbage and tomatoes."

"All by hisself?" Alex persists.

"Or maybe she has company to help her?" Mrs. Tully suggests.

"Uh-uh, all by myself. 'Then I'll do it by myself,'" Alex quotes, on his way to the bookshelf. "All by myself said the little red hen!" He hugs the book as he brings it to his teacher, then pushes it into her hands.

In the darkened room at naptime eight sleepy toddlers listen to the familiar question. "Who will help me plant this seed?" and are asleep before the cat, the dog, and the duck receive their comeuppance. Later, when Alex's mother picks him up, he will tell her, "Those guys didn't want to help the little red hen," and she answers, "But not my baby, right?"

In Mrs. Tully's room, one is pulled along by a comforting and continuing narrative in word, motion, book, and song. She knows the landscape well, having followed it back to her earliest memories. I have come to watch the youngest storytellers, but what I see is the reincarnation of home and the invention of theater.

Lillian Tully does not use the word "theater," but she talks about home and community. "When my babies do their stories, that's when they really see each other," she says as we leave the sleeping children in Connie's care. "That's what we need to go after in school, the seeing and the listening to each other."

We continue our conversation in Lillian's office, on a first-name basis now. "There's a point I want to make," she says, looking at the clock. "I've got just a short time to do it in so it'll sound like I'm giving a speech. Sorry if I do."

"Go ahead," I laugh. "My husband tells me I often sound that way. It must go with the territory."

"Okay then. When you see Alex on the playground, for example, he'll be running in the opposite direction of everyone else. He'll yell, 'Chase me, chase me,' and no one pays attention. Compare that to what happened when he told his Mama story. They looked at him and said his words. And then he returned the favor. Amazing, isn't it? The beginning of an *us*. A real community. Everything eventually gets included, even the little red hen, all by 'hisself' and myself."

Lillian is no longer self-conscious about her speech making. "Would this sort of thing happen if he didn't realize where stories come from? You've got to wonder about that. And take Valerie, there's another good example. Only with her it's *The Runaway Bunny*."

I burst out laughing. "So that's what she was referring to! I was writing in my notebook before and she said to me, 'Then I'll be your pencil if you do that.'"

"Exactly!" Lillian is as animated as her children on the playground. "Listen to this! Once I was telling the twos about my grandpa's bees and how one of my brothers always tried to take their honey and got stung every time. So Valerie said, 'If he takes the honey then I'll be the mama bee and I'll *give* him the honey.' Imagine this from a child not even three, using one story to get at another."

"It's what we try to get much older children to do," I say, "and here's your Valerie an expert at two." Now it's my turn to give a speech. "Plain and simple, your children are practicing logical thinking. When adults do it we say they're having an intellectual discussion, but when young children put all this stuff together people barely notice."

"Or they think it's cute or funny," Lillian says. "You're right, it is intellectual. I'm always afraid to use that word, but you watch them. Now, whenever someone picks up *The Runaway Bunny* it seems like another child will remind us that Valerie is the mama bee even though there's no mama bee in the book, only a mother rabbit."

The mother rabbit in Margaret Wise Brown's book listens to her child's fantasies and provides a gently protective response to each one, not unlike what Lillian does herself. "'If you become a fish in a trout stream,' says the mother rabbit, 'I will become a fisherman and fish for you.'"

In Mrs. Tully's room, children as young as two understand that Valerie can be a mama bee in the same way the mother rabbit pretends to be a fisherman or pretends to be the wind blowing on her baby rabbit while he pretends to be a sailboat.

It is a literary network, propelled by the need children have to connect themselves to one another through their play and stories. Lillian calls it community, but it is also theater.

Nothing is what it seems to be in this theater of the young. Alex is the first to wake from his nap. He drags his blanket to the doll corner and stirs a large spoon in a small pot on the stove. Valerie enters next and hands him the raggedy-eared bunny he left on his cot, then retrieves a doll from under the crib. She stands beside Alex hugging her doll and the two children gaze into each other's eyes. The unspoken words seem to be, "Where's Mama?"

The threes, fours, and fives, called the olders, are in two large rooms on the other side of a wide hallway. Both rooms, like those occupied by the twos, could have been furnished out of a Victorian attic. Antique cradles large enough for pretend babies mix with an odd assortment of oak pieces long ago painted with ivy and rose buds. The blocks are the dark solid kind of an earlier era, and the wooden trucks seem like museum pieces. All this, and the silk scarves draped in unexpected places, gives the rooms a fairy-tale quality.

Lillian alternates her mornings and afternoons between the twos and the olders. There are several other adults in each group, including parents who come in on a regular basis, but it is Lillian herself who keeps the threads of community visible.

At lunch with the olders she says, "Alex told a one-word story this morning. One word is all."

"What is it?"

"Mama. Just mama. Everyone wanted to do his story."

"Did my sister?" Mike asks.

"Yes, Angela was first. Then Emily and Stuart and Sidney and Simone and Valerie and Lamar." The olders smile, knowing that no one is left out.

I remember feeling this way when I was a child and a Greek girl thrilled me by reeling off the names of her nine siblings. Whenever I said to Frieda, "Tell me your brothers and sisters," she did so, willingly, never asking me why. Somehow this helped ease my anxieties in school. No one was left out.

After lunch, the olders resume their morning play. Some go directly into block structures left standing from before and others head for the sand or water tables and the doll corner. "I'm the big sister this time, don't forget," and "Pretend the boat is sinking but I know what to do" are the sorts of messages the children send one another. These are the connections they make on their own, without the teachers' becoming involved.

Half a dozen children take seats around a large table in the center of the room. They are the crayoners and paper cutters, the Lego builders, puzzle workers, and book "readers," all of them telling something to somebody.

"Uppy uppy crash-o! Guess who's inside?"

"Who?"

"Uppy uppy crash-o! Who you think's in here?"

"Who?"

"This one's the bad guy. This is the bullets. Puh! Puh! Puh!"

"Do it on mine, okay?"

"I can't, I'm invisible."

"Here's the princess, in the window."

"Mine don't have a princess. This is a cat."

Is anyone listening? I watch the children carefully: not only do they appear to respond to at least half the things they hear, they also manage to attend to the storytellers. For this is, above all, the story table, an identity made clear by the fact that the teacher repeats the storytellers' words as she writes them.

Today Lillian is the scribe. "I love being the one who writes down the stories," she tells me later. "When I can't be here, if I have to meet with a parent or teacher, then someone else takes down the stories. But the olders bring them to me the minute I return. Sometimes we'll act them out on the spot. The children are telling me, 'This is what happened while you were gone.' Or maybe it's more like, 'Quick, give me the attention you gave to someone else when you weren't here with me.'"

I watch Lillian now as she waits for Allegra to speak. "This is your very first story," she whispers to the silent child beside her. Allegra is a newcomer to the center and visibly unsure of her place. She looked around to see if someone else wanted her chair before she sat down and she changed her mind three times before signing her name on the list of those who want to tell a story to Lillian. Finally she is ready, and the subject of her story is one I myself might have chosen when I was a schoolchild if we'd had such a thing as storytelling.

Allegra's voice is high pitched and barely audible. "Once upon a time there was a girl and no one noticed." What a remarkable beginning to a four-year-old's story. Lillian moves closer, echoing Allegra's words in low and musical tones, a cello accompanying the flute.

"Then someone noticed," Allegra continues, faster and louder, as if she wants to get all the words out before Lillian repeats them. "But then someone tells her she's the real one, but she can't understand, but someone noticed how she feels. She feels sad."

Lillian pronounces Allegra's final words slowly and everyone looks up. Their teacher's voice seems to be sending them a signal. Across the table, Thea has been turning the pages of a book as she observes the scene. Her eyes move from Allegra to the book and back to Allegra.

The book is *A Chair for My Mother* by Vera B. Williams, about a little girl, her mother, and her grandmother who are saving their money in a big glass jar to buy a red chair covered with pink roses. Then, when the girl's mother comes home tired every night from her waitress job, she will have a beautiful soft chair to sit in. When I first read this book to my kindergarten class, they were visibly moved by the demonstrations of kindness and love on every page. They insisted I reread the book immediately and someone said, "I'm gonna be that girl."

When it is Thea's turn to tell a story, she appears to enter into a conversation with both Allegra and the girl in the book. "Once upon a time," Thea says, using Allegra's opening line, "no one noticed. Then the little girl noticed a pink flower." Allegra does not look up but her face reddens and she begins to draw a pink flower.

"It was on a red chair with pink roses. It was her chair but she didn't notice." Allegra presses hard on her crayon, making the pink flower a darker shade.

"Then the girl noticed the red chair and it got more pinker and also pink roses on her dress and the little girl was happy because it was the same pink roses on the chair."

As Thea connects the girl in Allegra's story to the one in her own and both to the heroic girl who helps her mother buy a red chair with pink roses, every child at the table understands that Allegra has been officially welcomed into the group. Later, when the stories are acted out, those who are presently occupied in other parts of the room will also be informed that Allegra is a someone who must be noticed.

Without the habit of doing stories, how would these subtleties be expressed in such public detail? Of course there are always elements of the individual drama played out at various times all over the classroom. One can easily imagine a group of children drawing flowers together or even pretending to be flower girls in the doll corner. But the intense interplay of recorded responses I have just witnessed is inconceivable without the structure begun at the story table.

🌿 The olders act their stories out on a rug in the block area. This requires a total block cleanup before the rug can become a stage. The usual griping that accompanies the dismantling of boats and army bases is not heard; the children are eager to do their stories.

Allegra sits at the edge of the rug trying to make herself invisible. When Lillian calls her name and receives no response but a lowered head, she walks over to Allegra and kneels in front of her. "Your story is next, honey." Allegra shakes her head.

"How about if we do your story and you just watch, is that okay?" Allegra does not say no, and the narration begins. The actors come forward, one by one around the rug, taking their parts. Jenny is "the girl no one notices" and Deepak will be the person who says, "You're the real one."

"Once upon a time there was a little girl and no one noticed," Lillian reads, and the children turn away or cover their eyes. "Then someone noticed." Now a number of children wave hello and call out a variety of greetings. "Ha' ya doin'?" "Hey, man!" When Deepak says "You're the real one," he moves toward Allegra but then remembers that Jenny is playing the role.

Throughout the production, in fact, the audience and actors watch Allegra. It is her story no matter who acts it out. Had the action taken place in the doll corner and had Allegra similarly refused to participate, her connection to the event would have been overlooked and forgotten. The difference between the doll corner and the stage is the difference between a private conversation and a public discussion of personal matters that concern the entire community.

Thea's story will be acted out next. After two years with Lillian, she knows how to give stage directions. Everyone is to enter the stage as a dark pink rose. "You too, Allegra," she says hopefully but is not discouraged when Allegra again chooses to remain alone on the edge of the rug. "Stand like this," Thea instructs the actors, framing her face with outstretched fingers. "When I touch you with my magic, come alive."

In spite of herself, Allegra has begun to watch her classmates. When Thea tells everyone to sit on "the big red chair with dark pink pink" it appears for a moment that Allegra will be tempted to step into the fantasy. But this is not to be the day she joins the others. Sometimes a community reaches out before an individual is ready to respond. Children understand this and willingly fill in the empty spaces when they perceive someone's struggle.

I remember a girl named Serena who panicked when she saw an empty chair at a table or realized we were about to act out a story with only one character. She would cry and run out of the room or hide under a table. Her classmates did not find this behavior odd; they made certain to remove the offending chair and reminded one another to have at least two characters in a story.

Allegra's classmates react in a similar way, perhaps even going a step further. When Thea, later, brings Lillian "the red chair book" to read, she calls it Allegra's book, though it is Thea herself who has uncovered the magic in its pages. Such is the potential of theater to discover pathways to an elusive character.

Community is seen and felt when memory and fantasy weave us into a common story. Language meets action and we begin to penetrate the walls that divide us. The effect is striking among the twos but even more pronounced with the olders, whom I visit during the remainder of the school day. I have forgotten how it feels to spend the day inside a repertory theater; I have forgotten the power released in young children who are deeply committed to telling and acting out stories.

But what I have most forgotten are the difficulties faced by the teacher as she attempts to orchestrate the amazing array of social and intellectual impulses into that harmonious whole we would like the classroom to become. "We know by experience itself," wrote a sixteenth-century scholar and teacher named Roger Ascham, "that it is a marvelous pain to find out but a short way by long wandering." For Lillian the short way is clearly marked. "When my babies do their stories," she had told me, "they really see each other. That's what we need to go after in school, the seeing and the listening to each other."

🌿 A week passes and I cannot stop thinking about Alex and Allegra. Their stories reverberate in distant echoes, slipping into my solitary walks and journal pages. The Mama story and the girl no one noticed follow me around with the soulful image of my yellow Labrador retriever as he waits for me to open the door and take him somewhere. I call Lillian and invite myself back.

On this day, however, Alex does not have a story for Lillian. His mother, Maddie Parish, has come to assist the teachers and he seldom leaves her side. She is pregnant and moves slowly. He sits on her lap at story time and she does not urge him to join the others.

When the story acting is over, Alex brings *The Little Red Hen* to his mother for a private reading. They settle into an overstuffed chair by the corner window and turn the pages slowly. Alex is the little red hen. "Who will help me cut the wheat?" he says and his mother replies in a squeaky voice, "'Not I, says the cat,' 'Not I, says the dog,' 'Not I, says the duck.'"

Alex returns to the first page, ready to begin again. "Would you like me to write down a story for you, honey?" his mother asks. "About the little red hen?" But Alex shakes his head and pretends to write on her arm.

"Now, let's see what your story is about. Once there was a good little boy name of Alex and he was so good the little red hen gave him all the cookies." Alex's fingers go into his mouth and he snuggles dreamily into the small space on his mother's lap not taken up by his soon-to-be-born sibling. Mrs. Parish places his hand where the baby is moving and Alex seems only mildly interested. My own curiosity is greater but the scene is too intimate and I turn away.

I have the impression that Mrs. Parish is shy with everyone except Alex, but at the snack table she surprises me, launching immediately into a story about a little girl on a big mountain. "Who might that be, I wonder?" she asks, pouring the juice. "It's me, that's who. Alex's mommy. You kids call me Mrs. Parish but I was Maddie back then. And I always called it *my* mountain because as far as I could see there was no other house around. Only us. So it was my mountain."

Mrs. Parish wipes up a spill and refills the cup without interrupting her narrative. "One day my little wagon began to roll down the road because I forgot to put it behind the fence. I began yelling, 'Stop, stop,' at the wagon but it wouldn't pay attention."

Alex leaves his chair and stands at his mother's side. "Bad wagon," he says, stroking her arm.

"Don't worry, baby. Just then my daddy came along—that's your Grandpa George—he came along with a bundle of firewood on his back. He grabbed up the wagon and gave it a good scolding. 'What kind of friend are you? Maddie told you to stop, didn't she?' Then my daddy lifted it by the handle and carried it back to me."

"Where the wagon at?" Alex wants to know.

"Your grandpa still has it far as I know. Next time we visit we'll ask about it."

"Stop wagon!" Alex rehearses. "Stop by myself!" The others begin to chant "Stop wagon," all except Mike, who is visiting from the olders. He has a question for Mrs. Parish. "Is that mountain in Chicago?"

"Uh-uh, honey, it's way down in North Carolina, pretty far from here. That's where Alex's people come from. Have you ever seen a mountain?"

"Me and Angela live in Chicago," Mike replies. "I don't know if I saw a mountain."

"Oh, you'd know it all right. It goes up, up, up, higher than a downtown building mostly. When you're bigger you'll get to see a mountain for sure."

Mike looks at his sister, Angela, and says, "I'm already bigger."

Back in his own classroom, Mike tells a mountain story. "There was a little rabbit and he didn't know what is a mountain. So he walked up and up and it was a mountain. But he rolled down. So he cried to get up. Then came a big tall man that was his daddy and carried him up the big tall mountain."

"This reminds me of Mrs. Parish's mountain," Lillian says. "Do you want to take your story over to the twos and show it to her? She'll be there a while longer today."

"My mountain's in Chicago," Mike says, on his way out. He takes Mitya with him because Mitya has made a picture of a mountain. It would not surprise me if the mountain theme is borrowed by others; one cannot predict which ideas will take hold of the children's imaginations and become part of the lingua franca. Watching the process by which a group of children create their own narrative symbols was always an exciting part of teaching for me. Who else but the classroom teacher can follow the stories day by day and try to piece the puzzle together?

Even so, in Mrs. Tully's room the storytelling network is so strong, I might be able to latch on to a number of strands. "May I come again?" I ask Lillian.

"How 'bout tomorrow?" she says and we both laugh. "What I mean is, please come any time." Then she points to my notebook. "You won't identify us, will you?"

"Absolutely not. That's important to me too, you know."

"I'm a private person," Lillian tells me. "Maybe too much so. It's only with the kids and their families I can open up. And I don't favor putting them on display. Anyway, you're mainly interested in the stories, right? That doesn't need names or places. Wally wasn't his real name, was it?" She was referring to a former kindergartner of mine, about whom I wrote a book.

"No, I don't use real names. The stories and discussions have to come across on their own."

"Speaking of Wally," she says, looking at me doubtfully, "I wonder . . ."

"You wonder what?"

"Well, you've heard so many stories. I mean your books are filled with them. So why us?"

I have already seen the question in her eyes. "But I haven't heard *your* stories or your children's. I've never heard a Mama story or a no-one-noticed story or one about a rabbit who can't get up the mountain. Besides that, and maybe this will surprise you, I don't know many people I can talk to about stories the way we do. People who do the stories every day and absolutely will burst if they can't talk about them and wonder about them. Maybe this and maybe that. Believe it or not, no one is better than you are at this."

"Grandpa was, for one. You should have heard him. He'd never let go of a story. Once he told us that we're all just poor wandering souls looking for someone to tell our stories to and that as long as he's around he'd hang on to anything we tell him and keep it alive."

The telephone rings and Lillian excuses herself to talk to a parent. We've established the fact that I will come back, though my reasons may not sound convincing enough for Lillian. If I told her the truth, she'd pull back in self-consciousness. I need Lillian Tully for those teachers and parents who tell me how much they want to do the stories but cannot find the time. Perhaps she can show them the ways in which storytelling extends and deepens the classroom experience. At the very least, she may help us remember our own stories.

"We're like the gumbo stew Mama kept bubbling on the stove," Lillian says. It is six-thirty, the beginning of her school day and an hour before the children start to arrive. "Everything she put in the pot made the gumbo more delicious."

I have asked Lillian to describe her center, and the gumbo image seems exactly right. "It's true of my own family as well," she continues. "I'm black, from Louisiana. Bernie, my husband, is white, from New Jersey. Our two girls, both adopted, combine Hispanic, Indian, and African backgrounds. Like Mama said, the more you add, the better it gets."

Her school population is even more diverse. For some, English is a second or third language, and

Lillian is always looking for teachers who are fluent in one or more of the home languages. "Bernie knows French and some Russian. And we're both studying Spanish. When the public schools are off— he's a fifth-grade teacher, did I mention that?—he'll come help us, with his toolbox and pocket dictionaries. If we could afford it, he'd teach here all the time. As it is, the reason we're able to keep going is because the church lets us use these rooms for practically nothing and we all work here for less than we could make somewhere else."

Her husband manages to stop by several times a week after his school day is over. With both their children in college, he no longer has to rush home. I remind Lillian of the board game he was constructing for Mitya, a four-year-old Russian boy, during my first visit. It was printed in Russian and English and the point was to bring each animal to the Moscow Zoo.

"Wasn't that a great game?" Lillian says. "Did you notice that the boy in the zookeeper's cap holding the cat is Mitya?" Apparently I had overlooked the most important symbol in the game. The children and teachers understood why the cat had to be there, but an outsider cannot hope to capture all the clues.

Lillian shuffles through a drawer of papers. "Mitya misses his cat so much. Here's a typical story of his. 'Cat is where? Meemya is Moscow.' You see, his reason for telling a story is so he can talk about his cat in Moscow. Sure, he could just *tell* us about Meemya the cat. But when he sees us write it down and then we act it out, we *live* the experience with him."

"He brings you all home to Moscow."

"And he feels more at home here. Alex hangs around Mitya a lot, you may have noticed, and he actually calls him 'Moscow.' Sometimes, in fact, Mitya will call Alex 'Aleksei.' Bernie says it's sort of like 'little brother.'"

Lillian begins to cut various shapes out of yellow, blue, and red tissue paper, then I take a few sheets and do the same. Christine, a teacher in the olders' class, has a project in mind, and Lillian offered to help with some of the preparations. This sort of busywork is useful in a rambling conversation such as ours. "What about you, Lillian? Did you feel at home when you were in school?"

My question causes her to frown. "I hated school. It was a very punitive place. It didn't personally affect me as much as it did my brothers, but none of us liked school. We all wanted to stay home with Grandpa."

"Your grandfather?"

"Grandpa took care of us. Me, my brothers, and my cousins. Our mothers and fathers worked and Grandma too, but Grandpa had lost a leg in a farm accident and he couldn't work anymore. You might say he ran a childcare center for us. He fed us, kept us clean, played with us, watched us play, settled our fights and wiped our tears, and mainly, it seems to me now, he told us stories. Stories, stories, all day long. I mean, that man had a story for everything!"

"But Lillian, this sounds like your own job description. It's what I see you do."

"That's the point, I guess. When I went into teaching I had this image of a porch full of cousins playing on the steps, hanging over the railings, listening to Grandpa's stories and making up our own. He even got us to write them down. See, school didn't begin until first grade in our town."

"He taught you to read and write?"

"No, no, hardly that. He was pretty self-conscious about reading out loud and about his spelling. He didn't get much schooling, you know, as a sharecropper's child. No, he wanted us to read to him. So we just sort of figured out how to do it, I guess. And Grandpa always connected storytelling to reading. 'That's a good story,' he'd tell us. 'Write it down for me so I can have something good to read while you're in school. Then I won't be so lonely.'"

"Then that idea, about stories making a child feel less lonely, that comes from your grandfather."

"I guess it does. The older cousins helped the younger ones write down their stories and sometimes we'd act them out for Grandpa. It was part of our play. We pretended school and it was a lot better than real school ever was."

She shakes her head mournfully. "When I started teaching in a public school, there was hardly a minute for play and stories. We were in straightjackets, so tight, so partitioned off from each other. Our principal didn't have a clue about how to make kids happy in school. I was becoming desperate. I kept thinking about Grandpa's porch. It was driving me crazy, there in front of my eyes all the time."

"Was that when you opened your own school?"

"Not right away. First I began taking just a few children into my home, to keep my own babies company. But our place was too small. Then, glory be, when our girls went off to kindergarten and first grade, I found out I could have these wonderful big rooms rent-free from my church. We only needed to pay the custodian for his extra hours. One of the deacons helped us get a small grant to make repairs and alterations, in exchange for taking in his grand-child. Without all this help we couldn't stay small as we are. That's so important. We must stay small."

"I agree, Lillian. You couldn't do what you do in a larger school. You couldn't teach in both groups and do the stories. To me, what you've got here is a sort of expanded home schooling."

"Home-porch-schooling, you mean. Which re-minds me, I never did the acting part of storytelling in school until I read about Wally, but we used to do it on the porch for Grandpa all the time. I just didn't think about it for the classroom and now it's the thing I would not give up for anything."

"You'd have come to it on your own," I assure her. "I never had a porch full of cousins and my grand-father felt too much a stranger to tell us his stories. He told them to the old men he met in the park near our apartment, immigrants like himself, but not to us. He must have figured the stories wouldn't mean much to us. Maybe the language barrier seemed too great or he thought the stories were too sad. Or maybe we didn't stick around long enough to give him a chance. Anyway, we didn't know his stories and he didn't know ours."

"Where did your grandfather come from?"

"They called it a shtetl, a little village, in Russia, smaller than your grandfather's town in Louisiana."

"My grandfather still had his own ground under him and yours didn't. I bet that's why he couldn't tell his stories to you. I want our kids to feel that school is their own ground. Did it ever get to be that way for Wally?"

"I think it was too late. By the time he came into kindergarten he was always expecting to be punished. This was the way his daycare handled problems. They had told us in advance that we were getting a bad boy. It helped a lot when I got rid of the time-out chair. And, by the way, being in a mostly white school for the first time must have come as a real shock to Wally. That in itself would make him feel lonely."

Lillian reacts quickly. "Hold on a minute! I went to an all-black school and I was scared and lonely all the time."

"What made it so scary for you?"

"People's anger. The anger of teachers toward certain kids. It was always there. Someone was always about to be punished. It was never me but that didn't matter. I remember holding my breath when the teacher yelled at someone or did worse. It might as well have been me."

Lillian's words mirror my own despair in the face of a teacher's anger although, as in her case, it was never directed at me. But I felt equally threatened when a stuttering child was ridiculed by children, certain that I would be the next to stutter and feel ashamed. It took me many years as a teacher to understand that one child scorned is every child's humiliation.

The children begin to arrive at seven-thirty. Each child is brought into the classroom by a family member who is likely to spend a few moments in conversation with a teacher. Today the twos and threes do not separate easily from their parents. Lamar convinces his mother to read him a book and play a game before he will release her. Then he grabs a foam rubber ball from Emily and says, "Mine."

"My ball," she replies.

"My ball and my ball," they singsong, rolling it

back and forth until Emily suddenly departs with the ball.

Lamar moves to the play-dough bench. "My play-dough," he says, then changes his mind and goes to Lillian. "My story," he tells her. The morning activities are on their way.

Later in the morning, during the twos' naptime, we continue our conversation in Lillian's office. "It was clear to me, the first day, that no one was going to be punished here," I say. "But don't you think even your school can be scary for some children?"

"Allegra shivered if anyone came near her in the beginning," Lillian replies after a pause. "The family wanted to keep her at home, but her mother had to return to work."

"And yet she is able to tell this personal story about a girl no one notices. Weren't you surprised?"

The phone rings and Lillian gives directions to a student teacher coming in for an interview. When she hangs up she says, "Allegra tells her story because the rest of us do. You don't feel so scared when people are telling you stories. It's not only fear of being harmed that scares you. Being lonely, being afraid no one will come pick you up, being worried that no one likes you . . ."

"Or notices you."

"Right. But the thing is, all these scary things are less so if no one is being punished." The telephone rings again, a parent telling Lillian she's going to be late.

"Don't worry," Lillian says. "If you're not here when Bernie comes for me, we'll take Valerie home and you just pick her up there, okay?" Lillian writes herself a note, then returns to our conversation. "The public school I started teaching in was a punitive place—kids sent out in the hall, into a coat room, to the principal's office. That's the way problems were handled. You get on a teacher's nerves—Bam! Out the door! Banishment. Believe me, that kind of place makes you go into hiding. It's not a place for telling stories. Or for learning."

The telephone rings twice more; the parents know it is naptime, when Lillian can take their calls. She is patient but brief as she answers their questions. She invites one parent to stop by early the next morning, on his way to work, so they can talk further.

"Where were we?" Lillian laughs. "Oh, yes, no place for telling stories. But when I made my home into a school the stories returned, and my fun in being a teacher. I worried about moving to these large quarters. Maybe the balance would change when we got bigger, not enough time with the children, that sort of thing. But so far it hasn't happened. Bernie keeps reminding me that there are still fewer children in the whole school than I had, as a public school teacher, in any one class."

"You can almost fit everyone on your grandfather's porch."

She grins at me. "He'd figure out a way to handle us all. At least that's my memory of him. It was just one of these old farmhouse porches that went all around to the back, all kinds of leftover pieces of furniture, cots along the sides in case someone needed to sleep out there, plenty of room for a person to stop by and gossip for a while." She looks through the doorway and laughs. "Sort of how these rooms look, I guess."

"I've seen porches like that from the train window when we'd come up here for a visit," I say, "the time we lived in New Orleans. Even speeding by, they looked like cozy places, especially to someone like me who'd never had a porch."

"I can tell you, we felt safe and happy there. I can't guarantee that the grownups did. There'd be plenty of worried late-night conversations we weren't supposed to hear. All I know is Grandpa looked happy and safe out there, waiting for us to get off the school bus. He'd have milk and cake ready for us, or maybe lemonade and buttered bread."

Alex runs into Lillian's office, his fuzzy blanket trailing behind. Without a word he climbs into her lap and closes his eyes. A moment later Stuart follows him. They look like shipwrecked sailors locating a lighthouse. Lillian gathers Alex's blanket around both boys and continues talking about her grandfather.

"'Well, now,' he'd call out. 'Abe Lincoln didn't have a bus to carry him to school!' This might be the way he'd greet us. He never inquired about school. He knew we'd eventually tell him what we wanted him to know. 'Abe and Sarah, now, they'd walk miles to get to school. That boy'd go anywhere if he could learn something. And he never forgot a story he heard either.' Then Grandpa would begin one of his stories even before we poured our milk."

"Sweeter honeysuckle," Alex murmurs from inside the blanket and Lillian gives him a squeeze. She points to a picture on the wall. "That's Grandpa before the accident."

She pauses while I go over to examine the photograph of a tall gray-haired man standing alongside a tractor. I recognize his smile. It's the one Lillian has when she's about to tell a story. "Sometimes I wondered if Grandpa invented some of those Lincoln stories, just to improve our behavior. Then I read similar accounts in Carl Sandburg when I was in college."

"Maybe that's where he got them," I say.

"I doubt it. Grandpa had very little schooling. But he must have been like Lincoln in that he never forgot a story and he always knew where to apply it."

Lillian rearranges the boys on her lap to make them more comfortable but they decide they've had enough lap sitting and are fully awake so she pours them some juice instead. "By the way, Grandpa told us all sorts of other stories, things that happened when he was a boy picking cotton, trying to fool the grownups, or maybe a funny mix-up when he and Grandma were first married. And lots and lots about his sisters and brothers. 'Now don't tell Uncle Herman I told you this but . . .'"

"What he telled you?" Alex wants to know. He is pushing a little car back and forth with Stuart.

Lillian bends down to give each boy a neck rub. "About Uncle Herman? Oh, Grandpa might recall the time Herman climbed up on the roof and wouldn't come down all night because he'd gotten into an argument about something being as easy as falling off a roof. Herman had insisted that falling off a roof wasn't easy, it was hard. So that boy just had to prove it. I think he was arguing with *his* grandpa. He stayed up there all night and he didn't fall off either. The joke was, it was a flat roof, the kind a person probably wouldn't fall off of. His grandfather had meant the other kind of roof, a high slanted roof. Now, look here, boys, I'll show you." She draws a picture of a pitched roof and then, next to it, the flat one with a boy sitting on it. Alex takes the drawing for his own and studies it while Lillian continues to talk. Valerie has come in from her nap and automatically reaches up for a place on her teacher's lap.

"Sometimes Grandpa'd be in a real serious mood and we'd hear stories from slavery days, mostly about the courage and loyalty of ordinary folks. Those stories made us sad and Grandpa didn't tell them too often."

She puts Valerie down gently and walks to the window. Several other twos have wandered into the office and crowd around Lillian, looking through the window with her. "The thing that happened was this," she continues, and though she is still talking to me she might as well be speaking to the children who now stare up at her, listening closely. "The moment a story began, whatever it was about, all the hurts and sorrows of the school day flew away like a puff of wind."

Alex holds up the sketch of two roofs, tracing their outlines as if he can feel the differences. He puts his finger on the boy sitting on the flat roof. "Herman," he says. "Say it again."

Lillian retells the Uncle Herman story to the children surrounding her. The little ones do look as if a puff of wind has blown away their sorrows.

Wally's stories did this for me. So often he was on the verge of doing something I was not going to like. Then he'd tell us a story and the cloud lifted, blown away by a puff of wind. Soon I found myself waiting for the stories instead of the disruptive behavior. And I waited for his remarkable explanations of how the world works, which of course were like his stories. "I'm going to be a mother lion when I grow up," he told us once. "The library has everything. Even magic. When I'm eight I can learn magic, that's how."

Lillian calls me at home that evening. "I've got to ask you something: how did Wally do in school? I mean, after he left you. That's something we wondered about when we read your book."

I usually manage to avoid an answer to this question, but I want Lillian to know. "Wally didn't last long in our school. His mother took him out after second grade and put him in a Catholic school near his house. But that didn't work out either. In fifth grade his mother sent him to live with his father's people in Georgia and he did much better. She joined him there. 'It was better for both of us,' she told me. 'It's family there. Wally could be appreciated.'"

"Didn't you tell her how much *you* appreciated him, that you wrote a book about him?"

"No, I didn't, Lillian. I never name the real children in a book. Sometimes a character might recognize herself or himself years later but it doesn't happen often."

Lillian was not to be distracted. "Getting back to Wally, don't you find it strange? I mean, the way he loved all those discussions, and the storytelling and acting and all. This kid actually gave you a new way of teaching and even a book, for heaven's sake. Why couldn't he make it at your school?" There is a pause and, even over the telephone, I sense Lillian's embarrassment. She is upset but probably feels it is not her place to criticize my school. "I mean, I'm just curious is all," she says mildly.

I have no answer that could satisfy her—or me. "No, he couldn't make it. He must have started feeling like a stranger again, too much in the wrong. His mom could see that there were so many complaints and hardly any compliments."

"I worry about this," Lillian admits, "when my kids leave the center. In fact, I'm trying to figure out how we can extend the program to include kindergarten, even first grade for a few children. Bernie and I talk about this a lot. We'd have to move to a bigger place and hire another teacher, something we can't afford to do without raising tuition and lowering salaries. That we are not prepared to do, and without the deal the church gives us, we'd go broke anyway. Still and all, it's a wonderful dream. I mean, imagine if your Wally had stayed with you a while longer."

My Wally. Out of an unremarkable gesture of mine intended to lighten one child's spirits came the certainty that every child has a continuing supply of stories—and, furthermore, that these stories must be acted out. A simple premise, yet one that would direct the next two decades of my teaching and writing life.

The sequence of events was this: one day, Wally, age five, dictated a story about a dinosaur "who smashed down a city and the people got mad and put him in jail." There was nothing unusual about the story or about a kindergarten teacher writing it down. Except for the fact that Wally, moments earlier, pretending to be a dinosaur, had knocked over several block buildings and was sent to the time-out chair by an angry teacher. Me.

I had sent him there automatically. Just as surely Wally and the children knew he would be sent there. The time-out chair belonged to a school scenario in which certain children had a starring role. But now, art and life had merged to illuminate a disturbing phenomenon.

I had been doing to the children what Wally did to the dinosaur. "The people got mad and put him in jail" was little different, it suddenly appeared to me, than a teacher sending a child to the time-out chair. I was pretending the procedure changed children for the better when I could see that everyone felt worse, those on the chair and the rest of us who watched the punishment.

The connection between Wally's fantasy and the chair called for more than the usual reading aloud of a child's story. I wanted Wally's position to be recognized in a more dramatic way. We would act out his story.

"Why are we doing this?" someone asked.

"Because Wally was sad, sitting on the chair." Further explanations were unnecessary. The children accepted the idea that telling a story and acting it out would make a person happy.

"How long you s'posed to stay in jail?" Wally was asked, the sort of question children ask each other when they play. With the time-out chair only the teacher knew how long a punishment was required to improve a child's behavior.

"Just maybe two minutes," Wally decided. "That's enough. Then he promised to be good so they let him go home and his mother was waiting." A Mama story after all.

The results of this singular piece of theater were immediate and lasting. Nearly everyone wanted to do a story "like Wally did" and our curriculum changed to include a new activity we called storytelling. Over the years there would be innovations and variations but the basic plan of dictating stories and acting them out on the same day continued. This was the children's own theater, of and for themselves. The rituals and identifying symbols of one class distinguished it from all others. The stories were its fingerprints.

Eventually I eliminated the time-out chair. Its existence pulled us apart whereas theater brought us together. But why can't we have both, I'd be asked by assistants and student teachers who perhaps felt more confident knowing a child could be removed when all else failed. I became convinced, however, that what failed was, in part, due to the presence of the time-out chair. It interfered with our faith in the effectiveness of rational solutions between people of goodwill. "Do this—or else!" is, simply put, not as reasonable to a child's ear as "Once upon a time there was a dinosaur and he was having a big problem."

The subject of punishment occasionally comes up at the teacher conferences I address, though in general people prefer not to talk about it. Recently I asked for a show of hands from those in the audience who make use of a time-out chair. Nearly everyone raised a hand. Then I asked, "How many of you see long-term changes in those who regularly occupy the chair?" Not one hand went up, causing a good deal of laughter. I decided to read a transcript of Wally's own assessment of the issue.

> *Wally:* In my old school, if you tore someone's picture you sat in the hallway all alone by yourself until you were good.
>
> *Teacher:* Did it make you good?
>
> *Wally:* Yes. Hey, you know what we did in the hallway? We tore off the pictures on the wall.
>
> *Teacher:* Then being out in the hallway didn't seem to make you good, did it?
>
> *Wally:* They didn't know it was us.

🌿 Lillian does not use a time-out chair or any other punishment. Her determination to find other ways to influence behavior sometimes puts her at odds with colleagues and even with a few parents, but she is adamant. "We were not punished at home," she states with finality. "At school, yes, all the time, but not at home. Grandpa wouldn't allow it and he was right."

I have been invited to the monthly meeting of faculty and parents. Lillian uses these informal evening sessions to explain her thinking about children, and she encourages everyone to have a say. The subject of punishment has come up tonight because one of the parents had urged a teacher in the center to spank his child "when necessary."

"Let's talk about this business of getting rough with kids in school, isolating them, yanking them around, even spanking, which goes on in some places, as you know. To talk about these things, I must begin with my grandfather. He had no quarrel with jailing criminals, mind you, but he saw nothing good ever coming out of being mean to kids. There was plenty of that when he was young, so he knew what it felt like. Probably most of you do too."

A father objects to Lillian's terminology. "I'm sorry, but I don't see it as being mean to stop your child from doing wrong."

"Absolutely," she responds quickly. "The question

is how you aim to accomplish this. Now I know some of you are wondering why I keep bringing my grandpa into these matters. The reason is, he's the one who formed my experience and this influences the way I run this school. So it's important that I explain his thinking."

She smiles warmly at the man who spoke. "I'm not shutting you up, Fred, and we do need to hear from you, but let me first set out my grandpa's approach. Believe me, it wasn't the usual way of handling misbehavior back then in our little town in Louisiana."

"Not in my town either," Fred laughs. "Or with my grandfather. We all learned to tiptoe around that gentleman. He'd just about used up his patience in this world."

"I know what you mean," Lillian says. "That's the way it was in our school, as if the grownups had used up all their patience—and maybe most of their humor and kindness as well. But Grandpa saw things differently. He aimed to get us *thinking*. He said it was stories that got him to think and he figured stories would do it for us. We'd be expected to improve our behavior as a result of seeing his disappointment *and* listening to his stories."

Lillian sips her coffee and looks around the room.

There are a dozen men and women present plus two sleeping infants, not a bad turnout for a small school. "Some of you know my brother, Petey," she says. "He grew up to be a pretty good lawyer right here in Chicago and I know he's helped out a few of you." She acknowledges those who are nodding their heads.

"Well, let me tell you, Grandpa's approach to these matters saved Petey's life. He was treated pretty harshly in school by the teachers and the principal. I'm not saying he didn't drive them crazy, but they managed to take the heart out of him every day. If he'd come home to the same treatment he'd be in prison now for sure."

The room is so quiet I can hear one of the babies breathing heavily. "I recall when even Grandpa would be too upset for a story. 'Just set there a while,' he'd say. 'Darned if y'all didn't blow every thought out of my mind with what you just did. Hold on. Something's bound to jump in again.' You know, sometimes this will happen when I'm with your kids. I'll ask them to wait until I think of a good story, just the way Grandpa did. How do I know it makes sense to do this? Because it made such good sense to us when Grandpa did it!"

The continued presence of her grandfather in her

life is comforting and reassuring to me, as it seems to be to these parents. Lillian's respect for him and the way he handled a porch full of cousins left in his care is superimposed on all her thinking about school.

"Could you give us an example of how this works in school?" a parent asks. Her name tag reads "Sherry Taylor, mother of Mike and Angela."

"Sure. I'll even use Mike if you don't mind." It is clear that Lillian knows Mrs. Taylor well enough to be sure she won't mind. "Okay. A few days ago, Mike purposely splashed black paint on another child's painting. We were all pretty shocked by the suddenness of this destructive act. It seemed to come from nowhere. Instead of blowing up and issuing some form of punishment, I told a story to everyone about one of Miranda's calves—Miranda was Grandpa's cow—one of her calves knocking over the pail of milk whenever she could. We figured she was jealous of us for taking her mama's milk, that Sarabeth had to drink her milk *first* before her mama got milked by one of us. The story was more elaborate than that, you know. Sarabeth ran away, that sort of thing. But here's what was important. All the children had to be involved with the story. They had to care about helping someone get over a bad time. No, we didn't find out what was bugging Mike, but the story about Sarabeth and the pail of milk somehow got translated into the paint he'd splashed on Jordan's picture. Sure, Mike helped clean up the mess, but what was important was he and Jordan still liked each other and no one had to feel guilty or scared because of someone being yelled at and punished. Now this approach comes right from Grandpa."

Lillian is aware that stories about her grandfather will not resolve the punishment issue. These stories do, however, help get people talking. Few of us present have not experienced the pain of punishment and the relief of forgiveness. Most people cannot imagine a childhood without punishment.

"We were raised strictly," a father stands up to say. "With a heavy hand. At the time I resented it, you bet I did, but now it makes sense to me. Maybe your grandpa didn't need to punish because the school did it for him. Is that possible? 'Good cop, bad cop' sort of thing? Seems to me punishment is part of growing up. Someone has to do it. I wouldn't hesitate to spank my kids when they disobey us. And we'll isolate them too. They have to earn the right to be with us."

These are harsh words, but Lillian looks at the

speaker kindly. "There are schools that feel as you do. We've all attended them and I've taught in them." She says no more at this time, willing to let the audience think about these opposing views.

Stuart's mother raises her hand. "My problem is that I get so mad sometimes, especially at my second grader, there's no way I could stop myself and tell a story. But I truly appreciate the fact that you're able to handle problems this way. After all, the kids are with you all day long."

Alex's mother has been moving around in the back of the room. "It really doesn't work," she calls out. "Being punished all the time doesn't work. My older sister, Lily, ran away when she was a teenager. She just gave up, you know? Lily was always in the wrong, at home and at school. I was so scared when she left and I've never gotten over it. Where do you think all those homeless kids come from? I won't do that to Alex or to the new baby when it comes. I'm learning a lot watching Mrs. Tully. I'm trying to get Alex's dad to visit so he can see a different way of being with children." She looks around at everyone. "You have to see how it's done. You can't explain it otherwise."

I think of little Maddie shouting "Stop!" after her

runaway wagon and her father carrying it up the mountain to his little girl. These are the stories she remembers and passes on to Alex and his classmates, not the times she was punished and made to feel sad.

Maddie Parish is right. This "different way of being with children" is best examined incident by incident. The next day I witness a scene that illustrates more about classroom discipline in ten minutes than many come across in an entire college course.

Samson has just thrown himself on top of Aaron, screaming and punching. The boys are so entangled I can't see which one is losing the battle, but Lillian has them apart before any harm is done.

"My, my," she says over the din. "Our Miranda would cry and cry if she saw you boys. Poor cow. And her milk would turn sour. Then Grandma and Grandpa wouldn't have milk for their coffee and they'd be annoyed with us and so we'd be annoyed with the chicks and, well, one thing always leads to another and Mama would have to run real quick to cover Miranda's ears."

"Why would she?" asks a tearful Samson in spite of himself. A story is about to be told. Lillian sits down on the piano bench and, before she begins, the space in front of her is suddenly filled with children.

"Okay, you're all thinking, now why would Miranda the cow have to have her ears covered just because my brothers are fighting? Well, Miranda liked a peaceful barn, you see. She couldn't bear it when Petey and Orin hurt each other, and her milk went as sour as a pickle. Being a cow, she didn't care who started the fight, but she was real proud of her sweet milk." Aaron and Samson have inched over to opposite sides of the rug but Lillian motions to them to come sit next to her.

"Moo, she say moo?" Alex has been tagging along after Lillian and is now in her lap, sucking on three fingers.

"She mooed real loud so her babies couldn't hear my brothers yell at each other. And she'd swish her tail every which way so they couldn't see Petey and Orin push each other. Miranda didn't want her own little ones to see us being mean and copy us. What if they got it in their minds to push a baby lamb or scare a new colt, the one that couldn't hardly stand yet? You can see that Miranda needed a peaceful barn. And we surely did want her sweet milk."

Lillian bends down to smooth Aaron's hair and

touch Samson's arm. "Now you know how it is with fighting, how everything gets out of hand and turned around. Pretty soon Grandma's yellow canary bird stopped singing and Jo-Jo the turtle hid his head in his shell and then Bella the goldfish swam under her stone bridge and wouldn't come out."

The children are impressed by the seriousness of these events. But now Lillian bursts out laughing. "I've got to tell you a funny thing, though. One time, when Grandma herself was doing the yelling at Grandpa for something he'd forgotten to do, *I* went over to Miranda and covered her ears and her eyes. That gave everyone a good laugh because I was just a little girl then."

"With ribbons on your head," Alex murmurs. Allegra reaches out to touch his tight little curls and keeps her hand there for a few moments. Suddenly the classroom seems a safer place.

Only now does Lillian refer to the fight between Aaron and Samson. "By the way, Samson, you were pretty angry before."

"That's 'cause he keeps on stealin' my car!"

"Not so your car!"

"And Aaron, you needed that car, did you? That's just what used to go on with Petey and Orin. They'd even fight over a stick. Why they'd . . . well, wait, I need you to help me show how mad they'd be. You boys grab at this Tinker Toy stick, okay? And let's the rest of us be Miranda . . ."

"And the canary bird!"

"Right. And Jo-Jo and Bella, too. Now, here comes Mama to cover our ears!"

Self-consciously, Aaron and Samson yank on the stick, the others mooing and holding their ears. Thea decides to caw like a crow, which brings on a fit of coughing. Then Miss Handleman, the student teacher, runs to get her a cup of water at which point the tug of war ends since everyone is watching Thea cough.

When Thea is finally able to stop, Lillian sighs. "There, the barn is peaceful again. We'll have sweet milk for lunch today."

"In Grandpa's coffee," says a breathless Thea.

The image of Miranda's peaceful barn conveys the message better than any lecture on cooperative behavior. The children are ready to like one another and move on, returning to their activities in a hopeful mood, as though something good has happened. Their teacher's story allowed them to imagine people and animals living together in harmony, sparing everyone the indignity of punishment and recrimination.

Lillian's stories have an ever ready cast of characters who arrive charmingly when the children, and perhaps Lillian herself, are most in need of them. There are Mama, of course, and the little girl with ribbons on her head, along with Grandpa, Grandma, and all those brothers and cousins. Then we have Miranda the cow, Jo-Jo the turtle, the yellow canary bird, Bella the goldfish, and probably others I haven't met yet.

"Where's your daddy at?" Dwayne once asked Lillian.

"He died when we were little," she explained. "We missed him a lot. We knew he'd been real sick and now he's in heaven."

"Oh, yeah, that's where my daddy's at too."

Lillian reads books over and over to the children whenever they ask or when she herself is in the mood. But it is when she begins a story of her own that invisible ties envelop the room, not unlike the effect achieved by the children's own stories.

As a teacher my earliest attempts to invent stories

coincided with the elimination of the time-out chair. One of my first stories, in fact, involved a time-out log that rolled into the river and could no longer be used to correct Ossie Beaver's behavior. When Mrs. Beaver moaned, "How shall we get that child to be good if we can't put him on the time-out log?" the forest animals were eager to give advice and so were the children in my class.

They liked my stories of Ossie Beaver's predicaments and almost any story I told seemed to improve their tolerance for one another's imperfections. But my stories lacked the conviction of a drama that has its roots in the storyteller's inner life.

Then, in my final decade of teaching, along came Magpie, a magical bird who knew me and knew my dreams as if we'd been together all along. Besides Magpie, there were Beatrix the witch, Princess Annabella and her father Prince Kareem, Princess Alexandra, and a runaway boy named Raymond. Overseeing them all in a place called the Kingdom of Tall Pines was the gentle, nonjudgmental Schoolmistress.

I recognized her immediately and with enormous gratitude; she was the teacher I had yearned after as a child. Her quick response to loneliness and rejection inspired me and strengthened my resolve. She was the teacher I wanted to be now. I was inventing characters, it would seem, for the purpose of improving my own behavior and fulfilling my fantasies. After all these years of watching the children act out their stories I was learning some of their secrets.

Unfortunately, when I retired from the classroom, Magpie retired with me. No matter how I tried to bring him back to the pages of my journal, the easy flow of fantasy was gone. Apparently I still needed that classroom of children doing their stories to prod me into doing mine.

Lillian and I have begun to write each other letters, sometimes only a sentence or two. "How does Miranda help Aaron and Samson become more agreeable?" I ask, leaving the note in a box on her desk. Her response goes into a basket next to it. "They understand Miranda's need for a peaceful barn better than me wanting a peaceful classroom."

Later, in another note, she adds, "Or, maybe, the idea of Miranda's sweet milk is so easy to apply: if the block play goes well, we say, 'Miranda's milk will be sweet today.'"

"What about this?" I offer in a return note. "When I think up a story, my anger is diffused. Stuart's mom said she was sometimes too angry for a story, but I'll bet it works the other way too. You can't stay mad while you're telling a story. But you don't find this out until you do it. It takes practice."

On the days I come we meet early to talk. This morning we are having a special treat: café au lait. "Because you lived so long in New Orleans," Lillian tells me, "and your heart is still there, I think."

She stirs a pot of milk, heating it just to the boiling point. Then she quickly removes it from the burner and, French drip pot in one hand and saucepan in the other, she pours the strong coffee and milk together into our cups. "Café au lait!" she announces.

Even her coffee comes with a story. "When Grandma visited her cousin in New Orleans, he took her to the place where he worked, the Café du Monde in the French Quarter." Lillian puts a teaspoon of honey in her coffee and in mine. "Grandma's special taste. Of course, her honey came from Grandpa's bees."

We each take another spoonful of honey and Lillian resumes her story. "Grandma couldn't be served out front, being black and all, so she and her cousin had their café au lait and sugared baguettes in the kitchen. 'The queen's parlor,' Grandma called it. From then on, Sundays before church Grandma gave herself that treat."

Lillian takes on the glow that accompanies so many of her childhood memories. "Years later, when we came along, we'd be allowed to have Grandma's coffee-milk with honey. 'Come into the queen's parlor,' she'd say, and if she felt up to it, she'd make honey buns too."

Café au lait had been part of my Sundays too. When my husband and I and, later, our two sons strolled around the French Quarter, we often stopped at the Café du Monde. It's possible, I suddenly realize, that Lillian's grandmother was sitting in the kitchen while we were being served in the open-air dining area. I wonder whether or not to mention this piece of my history but decide to leave the queen's parlor image undisturbed.

Lillian, however, does not need me to set the record straight. "Grandma was not a simpleton, by the way. She knew she was being humiliated in that

French Quarter kitchen. But she wasn't about to let *them* have the last word on *her!*"

🌿 Our letters begin to cover a lot of territory. The one I find in my basket at the end of the day makes me smile. "Do you still tell your Magpie stories? Haven't noticed any in your last two books."

"No I don't," I scribble on the back of her note. "That part of me ended when I stopped teaching." The next morning I am more expansive in a letter I post at the airport. I'll be away for two weeks.

"My last Magpie story," I write, "was on my final day of school. Schoolmistress decides to leave the Kingdom of Tall Pines and look for a place she has seen in her dreams where there are children but no schoolteacher. She is certain she must go there and Magpie and Beatrix insist on going with her. They promise to return to the Kingdom of Tall Pines but it hasn't happened yet."

As the plane lifts off, a story begins to form. Beatrix is digging a hole and finds a tiny red chair. The connection to Thea is clear enough, but this chair belongs to little Prince Orange Flower, a character from a long ago story who lives in a cactus flower. Magpie had once rescued him from the Great Golden Eagle by a clever ruse, yet how would the chair find its way into one of Beatrix's holes?

And the hole itself, why is Beatrix digging it? My children would have laughed at that one. Beatrix, poor thing, was always digging holes in the hopes of trapping an unsuspecting schoolchild on her way home from school. Beatrix was certain she could make friends this way, though Magpie had warned her again and again that friendship does not happen in traps.

Magpie ought to warn me as well; with no classroom of children waiting to hear about him and Beatrix I am not likely to trap my story. I allow myself a moment of regret, then turn to a fresh page in my journal and recall a scene that rivals any I could invent for Magpie.

Mitya, Dwayne, and Mike have built a boat that is sinking in the Moscow River. "Deep water floating!" Mike yells. "We're sinking!"

Dwayne waves his arms wildly and knocks down a block. "We drownded but I saved you. Oh no! We're sinking again! Nine-one-one!"

Thea walks by holding Angela's hand. "We'll save you, me and Angela."

She tugs briefly on invisible ropes and puts the overturned block in place. "There! We saved you."

"Is very strong ladies," Mitya says admiringly as the girls head into the doll corner.

We stand at the double sink washing paint jars when Lillian turns to me and says, "You do like us, don't you." It is a statement of fact, not a question.

The last child has been picked up and Lillian is waiting for Bernie. "It's important to me that you do," she goes on. "You call us teachers. We're a school to you. Everyone here appreciates that. Most people will say 'daycare worker,' you know, as if we're less than teachers and this is not a real school. I think it's because we work for such low pay. Even most grade school and high school teachers don't take us seriously. Bernie says the teaching here is on a par with what you'll find in a good classroom at any level. But to the outside world we don't count for much."

I have finally seen Lillian when she is too angry for a story. She concentrates on the paint jars for the next few minutes and then her face relaxes. "Anyway, back to important things. As Grandpa would say, 'Let's jump back into the water.'"

"Meaning?"

"Probably it referred to the runaway slaves covering their tracks by taking to the water. That's what Grandpa figured, sort of get back to what matters and don't dwell on what others are worrying us about."

"Okay, I agree. Let's jump into the Moscow River and talk about Mitya. How did he and Alex become so close?"

"It happened almost instantly," Lillian says. "Alex was visiting the olders one time when Mitya did a story about his cat Meemya. There couldn't have been two English words in the story, but Alex began to meow for all he was worth and wouldn't come out of the center of the rug. He just kept meowing until Mitya knelt down and petted him. From then on they acted like brothers—or cousins—and Alex began to call Mitya 'Moscow.'"

Lillian shows me a handmade book with "Where is Mitya?" crayoned on the cover. "One of Bernie's fifth graders did this for Mitya. See? Mitya is walking along the river with his grandmother, Babush. She took care of him while his parents worked and now she has the cat. These two pieces of information are very important if you want to think about Mitya. That and the Moscow River."

The book is quite clever; it's hard to believe a fifth-grade child did the whole thing. On every page someone asks, "Where is Mitya?" and at the bottom a tiny cat answers, "Mitya is in Chicago." On the last page the cat runs to a little boy and says, "There is Mitya!" The Moscow River flows through the book like a blue ribbon from page to page.

Lillian turns the pages slowly, savoring each cartoonlike character. "For a while, Mitya insisted we act out his book every day. 'Where is Mitya? He's in Chicago.' It became his mantra. Even the twos caught on to it. He's very fond of the twos, but Alex is his favorite. When Alex says 'Where's Mitya?' Mitya answers 'Where is Aleksei?' Then they grab each other and wrestle. Mitya is a very gentle boy, as you can see."

Were Lillian asked to write a lesson plan, how could she include all these important details? Come to think of it, if she taught in another school and had to follow a set curriculum, when would there be time for all these details to emerge?

"You know, Lillian, there isn't much that doesn't get acted out here and connected to something else. You really go far beyond where I've been."

"But don't forget, we're together all day, from early

until late. And we *stay* together. We have no take-out programs or special-area teachers to separate us, no gym or music to go to. We do everything ourselves, right here in these four rooms. We have easy access to one another, always. When Bernie tells me all the places his kids go to, I wonder how any simple conversation is ever finished, from beginning to end."

The frustrations come back to me in full force. "You can't imagine how bothersome this is! I'd always try to arrange the schedule so that just one day there would be no outside classes to attend. We called it our 'nothing-day' and it was like a day in the country. But I'll tell you what helped enormously on the other days: the storytelling and the acting. It kept us on track with one another."

Lillian laughs. "Bernie does the nothing-day thing too! Well, two afternoons actually. They call them 'home-free' times and they mainly do the stories, just the way we do. Of course, his kids write their own, although if someone needs help it's okay to dictate to Bernie or to another student. They even call them 'home-free stories.'"

"Are you talking about my home-free afternoon?" Bernie calls out, coming up the stairs.

"Afternoon? I told Vivian you have two of them."

"Not anymore. The computer lab just changed its schedule and we had to give up one of the home-free times. My kids are pretty upset even though they like going to computer lab. I suggested maybe they could do stories at home and we'll find time to act them out in class, but they said no, this is the kind of stuff you like to do on the spot with everyone."

"Have you told your fifth graders where the idea comes from? I mean, maybe some of them thought it was odd to be copying little children in a childcare center."

"You'd think so, wouldn't you? But that never happened. It started with these little stories we write for Lillian's kids, especially for someone like Mitya who doesn't speak English or a kid like Henry with a big speech problem. First I tell my students a story about each child, something that's important to the child, like Mitya with his cat. Well, after a while, a few of my kids wanted to do that sort of mini-story for themselves and have us act it out. The kids got hooked on it. Now we're trying to figure out how much we can shorten the time spent on it and still make it count. A girl named Marcia thinks that even a few stories a day accomplishes the purpose."

"What does she think the purpose is, I wonder."

"She told us. The purpose, according to her, is to

be *personal*. No, what she said was, to be *equally* personal."

They walk me to my car. "Remind me to tell you about Henry," Lillian says. "He's determined to do stories but it's nearly impossible to understand him. Still and all, he won't give up. And he won't let me escape until I get it down right. Before you know it, everyone around is trying to help."

"I've had a few like that," I say. "If I can locate something in an old journal I'll send it to you."

🌿 Driving home, I remember a three-year-old named Freddy. We called him the "simba-da boy" because nearly all his stories began with simba da. 'Da' we knew was daddy but simba was anybody's guess. It always seemed to mean something else and everything stopped while we tried to figure out Freddy's story. I didn't realize it at the time, but this daily group involvement was as much a symbol of who we were as any I could have devised.

🌿 "Dear Lillian, You are about to meet Freddy. I imagine he's a bit like your Henry. In those days I kept a tape recorder handy at all times. I was in nursery school then and, frankly, every word from these little ones seemed like gold to me. Freddy was a determined storyteller and became a classroom project. (By the way, have you ever used a tape recorder?)

Freddy: Simba da . . .

Teacher: Daddy is . . .?

Freddy: Simba da da.

Teacher: Daddy gives you the little car?

Freddy: Da uh uh simba.

   Paul: He means the space ship.

   Jilly: My doggy. That's what he's saying.

Freddy: No no. Some simba.

   Paul: The space ship. You 'member, Freddy? You was in it before?

Freddy: Simba da un. Wa-a-a.

   Jilly: The baby! The baby's going wa-wa?

Freddy: Ya ya! Da en me.

Teacher: Okay, so the baby is crying and you're the daddy. This is your story, right?

"Later when we act out his story, he kneels beside Jilly and rubs her back gently. By the way, before long

Jilly figured out what simba means. It's the word 'something.' Simple as that. See you on the tenth. Fondly, Vivian. P.S. The next year Freddy hardly needed anyone's help, but while he was struggling to be understood, this whole gestalt of storytelling and acting kept his spirits intact and ours too."

At the end of the week there is a letter from Lillian. "Dear Vivian, I made my first tape ever, of Henry at the sand table. The interesting thing here is that Henry is not even trying to tell a story. He's playing by himself with a little tiger. But I decided to put everything he does into a story just to see what happens."

Lillian: You're making a hill, Henry.

Henry: Mmm puh.

Lillian: A little boy made a hill. He pats it, pat pat pat.

Henry: Mmm puh!

Lillian: He pokes a hole in it and puts in a little tiger.

Henry: Me me too.

Lillian: The little boy lives there too.

Henry: Buh muh too. Mikey?

Mike: Okay. That kid and me we're going for a walk.

Henry: Un koo puh. Ten koo.

Teacher: To the park?

Mike: To school. We're going to school.

Henry: Yah, koo.

Lillian's letter continues: "Here is another scene, with Henry and Thea. I didn't tape it but I remember it pretty well because Henry says nothing. The reason I wrote it down is that Thea does what I was trying to do, only she goes much further. Let's face it, only another kid can go this far.

"Henry is playing with the medicine dropper in the doll corner, putting it into the doll's mouth. Thea runs in and starts asking him questions. 'Who are you supposed to be, Henry? Are you the dad? The mom? Oh, you're the doctor. Yeah, the baby is sick. Here, give the baby a shot. Do this! Henry, you're the doctor! I'm the mom. Mama la de da. Oh, thank you, doctor, the baby's all well again!'

"Well, before you know it, Henry *is* the doctor, scribbling on the prescription pad. Bernie says I should rent Thea out to other classrooms. Love, Lillian."

Before I am able to visit the center again, I receive another note from Lillian. "I'm practicing. This taping is practically hypnotic but, good Lord! how did you find the time? I have to limit myself to one small piece of tape a day or I won't get it transcribed. Anyway, this one is about Vassi, the girl from India. Have you noticed her much? She's easy to skip over, more so than Allegra, because Vassi won't talk to us. She talks at home but not to us. The great thing is, she plays in the doll corner all the time. Funny, but here is Thea doing her thing again and Vassi, notice, is not saying a word.

Thea: Hi, Mom. I'm going to the ball.

(Vassi gives her the red cape.)

Thea: Thanks, Mom. I'm Red Riding Hood.

Aaron: I'm the wolf dad.

Thea: Then you have to be in the woods. Then you come home and say, "How's the baby doing?"

Aaron: How's the baby doing?

Thea: No, say it to Mom.

Aaron: How's the baby doing?

Thea: Mom says fine. She's making you a birthday cake.

(Vassi holds up a chunk of play-dough.)

Aaron: It's a hunter's birthday cake. I'm a dad wolf that's a hunter.

(Vassi fixes a polka dot tie around his neck.)

Aaron: Thanks, Mom. Is that for the party? Okay, it's six o'clock. I just got home.

Thea: Tomorrow it's my birthday, don't forget.

"The play is interrupted because Aaron sees Samson and wants to play with him. Allegra has been watching the whole episode but wouldn't come in even though Thea asked her to be a sister. So here we have two girls: one tells a story but won't act in it and another one will take part in anyone's story but won't talk. Then there's Thea who puts it all together. Love, Lillian. P.S. And how about Aaron, the perfect wolf dad. All I can say is, thank heavens for the doll corner."

🍃 Lillian hands me a cup of instant coffee. "Sorry, no café au lait today. I'm all out of the French Market coffee." She makes amends with a Grandpa story.

"This bears somewhat on Vassi. My cousin Sally Bernice would sometimes get off the school bus in a rotten mood. Her teachers didn't like her and they let her know it. She didn't dare clam up in school, but when things got really bad she'd refuse to speak to us at home.

"Grandpa said it was okay and he saw to it that we left her alone. All the other grownups said he was spoiling her but we cousins knew better. Sally Bernice would have exploded if she couldn't have her way in this."

"The children feel this way about Vassi, don't they?" I ask. "From your tape it seems that no one thinks it's odd that Vassi won't talk."

"That's it. They assume Vassi is able to talk but simply doesn't want to, for her own good reasons. Anyway, I'm not quite as laid back as Grandpa. I've asked her father to spend time with us in school so she can hear him speaking to us in English. I think she might be confused about that. Her mom's been very sick so Vassi is with her grandmother quite a bit. Her dad and his mother talk together in Bengali. Maybe this is where the problem is. It's different than what was going on with Sally Bernice. But Grandpa's idea was that these matters will work out in time if we don't push and act as if something's wrong all the time. It easily applies to Vassi."

"Something else to thank your grandfather for. By the way, whatever happened to Sally Bernice?"

"She's a public health nurse in New Jersey, a single mom raising three nice kids by herself. People do grow up eventually, given some kindness and respect along the way. And, of course, in those days, we didn't feel every problem had to be identified and solved before first grade."

"I'll bet your grandfather had a Lincoln story for Sally Bernice," I say. "Abe was prone to his moods of silence, you know."

"Oh, yes. There was one story Grandpa told us where Mrs. Lincoln was trying to get his attention for over an hour and there he is stretched out on the rug reading a book while the boys are running all over the place. He doesn't answer her and finally she bursts out crying. Then he jumps up in surprise, feeling really terrible, apologizing. After which he goes right back to his book as if he's alone in the room. Sally Bernice was listening from her hideaway corner of the porch and she couldn't help herself. She burst out laughing. Then she remembered she's supposed to be angry, so she yelled at us, 'I ain't laughin' with y'all!'"

I fill our cups with soapy water and while I'm at it

wash everything in the sink. This morning I brought my own cup to school, with "Grandma" printed on it, a gift from my grandchildren that seems quite at home here in Mrs. Tully's room.

🌿 In the sandbox, Thea sticks four twigs into a cake of wet sand and offers it to Vassi. Her own cake also has four twigs and she feels this requires an explanation. "Does everyone realize I'm an older four on my birthday and Vassi is a younger four? You know why? Because Vassi already had her birthday and then mine came so I have to be older."

The children in the sandbox do not question Thea's reasoning. It is enough to be included in her "someone's birthday" game, played in a variety of ways. Today the number of candles is important. "How many candles are you?" she asks each one. Allegra answers "Six," Jordan says "Nine," and Dwayne, for unknown reasons, pushes in Vassi's cake.

She stares at him curiously, then carefully rebuilds her mold and adds three more twigs to the original four. "I'm seven," she says quietly. Vassi has spoken.

There are no clanging bells or flashing lights to herald the occasion. Only Allegra looks surprised.

The girl no one notices has noticed that the girl who never talks has spoken. I record the moment into my notebook: "Vassi's first school words, as far as I know, are 'I'm seven,' said after Dwayne spoils her birthday cake. Why choose now to speak?" Were I her teacher I'd have more to say. Probably every child in the sandbox can interpret the event better than I can.

Lillian is on her knees weeding the little garden on the other side of the playground. "You'll never guess what just happened," I whisper to her. "Vassi said two words! Dwayne knocked over her cake and she calmly remade it, put in seven sticks and said, 'I'm seven.'"

Lillian rises quickly, brushes the dirt from her knees and goes to tell the news to Martine, her assistant. Martine, in turn, walks to the slide to inform Celia, the aide, who looks around and, seeing no one else to tell, comes to me. "Guess what just happened!" she says. Even the sun appears to take note of the goings on in the playground, for it suddenly breaks through the clouds.

Lillian has resumed her weeding. "Why now?" I bend over to ask. "Did I miss something while I was gone?"

"Her dad came. Maybe that's it. He had lunch with us twice, in fact, and he was very talkative with the kids. He must have repeated every story Vassi ever brought home with her. The red chair story, Mike's rabbit trying to climb the mountain, Mitya's cat, the whole thing."

"That is some smart fellow!"

Lillian's next statement does not surprise me. "He's the father. A parent knows his child." Her faith in fathers and mothers, grandfathers and grandmothers is legendary. She believes in them and expects them to bring their wisdom into the classroom.

Furthermore, because the families know that Lillian believes in their children, they are willing to try to understand what is valued in Mrs. Tully's room. After a while it becomes natural for them to step along to the rhythm of the stories and play. When Alex's mother comes to pick him up and sees his tearful face, she knows exactly what to do, after giving him a hug and kiss. "Mitya!" she calls out, seeing him walk past the door. "Come tell me your cat's name. I keep forgetting."

Mitya runs in and grabs Alex's hand. "Cat is Meemya! Aleksei is being Meemya," he says. Wiping away a tear, Alex drops down on all fours, purring and pawing the air while Mitya rubs his neck.

❧   When E. B. White presented us with the world according to Charlotte, everything we wanted to know about friendship and loyalty was there for us to ponder in the Zuckerman barn. Yet, if we look closely, every classroom has its Charlotte, spinning "terrific" over a classmate's chair, and there is more than one Wilbur hoping for signs of love and belonging.

In Mrs. Tully's room it is Thea who most often takes on Charlotte's mantle and Allegra who plays Wilbur. However, in this world according to Thea, any one of us is likely to be given her attentive concern.

Allegra sits alone drawing rainbows. When she sees that I intend to join her, she looks around for Lillian, who is playing checkers with Mitya. Satisfied that her teacher is nearby, Allegra begins another band of color. "You're doing red next," Thea points out, moving her chair closer to Allegra. "Okay, then I'll do the red first, okay? Should I do red first? You have to tell me."

Allegra glances again at Lillian, then says, "Yes." Now Thea decides to spin her web over my chair. "Mrs. Paley could do a rainbow. She could do yellow first. Should she do yellow first, Allegra?"

Allegra looks relieved when I decide to speak for myself. "I think I *will* do a rainbow. Yellow you said, Thea? Yes, yellow is fine. I've never started with yellow before." Accepting the offer of Thea's yellow crayon, I take a piece of paper from the pile in the bin. "There, yellow is just right. Maybe next I'll do red."

Thea supervises our efforts with a watchful eye. "Do you re-a-lize that Allegra also does yellow first?" "Realize" is three distinct words. "And she does red next."

We seem to be speaking to each other in code. "And then?" I ask Allegra directly. "Does orange come after the red?" But it is Thea who responds. "See, Allegra mixes the yellow and also the red. La de da! Do you realize, really-a-lize how nice that looks?"

"It *is* nice, Allegra," I say, "when you make your own orange. Because every time you do, it looks a bit different."

Remarkably, Allegra turns to me and says, "I'm

adopted." She pauses, then rattles off the rest of what she wants to say in one breath. "But not Melanie because she comes from inside Mommy where you wish for babies but someone else wished for me but my mommy got that person's wish because she wished harder."

I manage to keep my voice calm. "It's the same in my family, Allegra. Our younger son is adopted, like you, and the older one came from inside me." I wait to see if Allegra has more to say but she concentrates on making the orange a darker shade.

I place my rainbow in front of her. "When you make the orange, Allegra, do you color the yellow first and then mix in the red, or do you do the red first and mix in the yellow?"

Allegra examines her own rainbow as though she is trying to remember. "You could first do yellow," she says, "if you want a light light orange. I'm first before Melanie because I'm older than the baby."

For a while we color together, three serious rainbow makers. Then Thea asks, "Why are you adopted, Allegra?"

Time stands still for me but Allegra has her answer ready. "I didn't have a mommy anymore and my mommy didn't have a baby so they finded me."

She looks at Thea as if waiting for a response but her friend is silent and they return to their rainbows.

"I know someone else who's adopted," I say, my heart thumping. "His name is Magpie. He's a big black and white bird." Magpie has flown out and there is no retreat.

"Allegra and me are black and white," Thea says.

"That's so, but Magpie has black and white feathers all together on himself. I guess that's how it might look if you and Allegra were hugging." The girls smile shyly at each other and I continue talking about Magpie.

"When Magpie was still in his shell, a big storm came and blew him right out of the nest into a soft pile of moss on the ground. Beatrix the witch found him and she kept him warm and safe until he hatched. She was lonely and she loved Magpie so she adopted him."

The girls have stopped coloring. "Is she a witch?" Thea asks. "A real one?"

"Beatrix *is* a real witch. But she's also a girl and she's Magpie's friend. Are you wondering if she's a good witch? Well, Magpie thinks she's not very different than Princess Alexandra, Princess Annabella, or Raymond. They are also his friends. Most of the time Beatrix is quite nice but then sometimes she wants everything for herself and Magpie tells her, 'Don't be like the mean old crow!'"

As my characters begin to awake from their long slumber, the lively and confident Princess Alexandra resembles Thea and the shy Annabella looks like Allegra. Mitya could be her father, Prince Kareem, and Dwayne, of course, must be Beatrix. He spoiled Vassi's cake in true Beatrix fashion, though there was little enough magic in his mischief. Unless we want to imagine his magical effect on Vassi.

"What does she do?" Thea has been asking me a question. "When she's mean, what does Beatrix do?"

"Nothing too bad, but being a witch she does know a bit of magic. Not as much as she probably should know. Her mother tells her it's because she'd always rather play than practice her magic."

"What does she do?" Thea wants more precise information about my young witch.

"Well, let's see now," I say, quickly forming a plot in my mind. "Here is what Beatrix will do. One day, Princess Alexandra had a birthday party and she forgot to invite Beatrix and Magpie. She invited all the children in her class, all the olders and all the youngers, and she invited Schoolmistress too. But then she got tired of writing invitations and, well, you see what happened."

"And her mother didn't help her," Thea says.

"Her mother, the queen, was too busy making the birthday cake. Anyway, poor Beatrix didn't get an invitation, or Magpie either. Now Magpie didn't care a bit. He told Beatrix that birds don't usually go to birthday parties."

"They don't," Thea confirms.

"Not witches neither," Allegra adds hastily.

"Maybe not, but Beatrix wanted to go. And she was unhappy. 'Tell Alexandra how you feel,' Magpie said, but Beatrix decided to do something mean instead. So she turned herself into a little brown moth with a yellow dot on one wing. Then she flew in through the open palace window and, poof! She made the birthday cake disappear. In a flash it was gone!"

The girls are alarmed. This seems more serious than when Dwayne smashed Vassi's cake in the sandbox which was ordinary naughtiness. "Luckily Magpie had followed Beatrix and heard everyone shouting, 'Where's the cake?'

"As soon as Magpie saw the brown moth with one yellow dot he knew who it was. 'Beatrix! You made

Alexandra cry!' Indeed, the tears were running down the princess's face. The queen looked as if she might cry too since she had spent all morning decorating the cake."

Thea is the acknowledged birthday cake expert. "The queen made pink flowers all around and a Barbie in the middle," she decides.

"Well, Beatrix hadn't even noticed what a fancy cake it was. But, besides that, she was not the sort of witch who wants to make children cry. So, she turned herself back into a girl, blinked her eyes three times, stamped her foot, and poof! The cake was back on its silver platter. Now it was Beatrix who felt like crying."

"Witches hardly ever cry," Thea says. Then she reconsiders. "Except if they're not invited."

"Anyway, there was no need for tears. When Alexandra saw Beatrix she ran up to her and took her hand. 'I'm so glad you came! We're just about to start 'Looby Loo.''"

"She's gonna be mean again," says Dwayne, on the floor behind us. He has been pushing a little car into my chair.

"Not this time. Uh, Dwayne, honey, please don't keep bumping my chair. Thank you much. No, indeed, Beatrix didn't even think about being mean now. When she's invited to play, she never feels mean."

Dwayne examines his car as if he hadn't realized what it was doing. Then he asks me about Magpie. "Does he play Looby Loo? With his wings?"

"Let me think. What was Magpie doing at the party? Oh, yes, Schoolmistress wanted to ask him about her yellow canary bird. It had stopped singing and she was worried. Magpie knew everything about birds, you see, even birds in cages."

"Mrs. Tully's grandma has a yellow canary bird," Thea reminds us, another detail I have borrowed along with the sandbox birthday cake. A children's book editor once told me, when I sent her a collection of Magpie stories hoping to have them published, "These really do belong in a classroom of children, everyone listening and picking at the fine points on the spot."

If Magpie has been waiting to find a classroom of fine-point pickers, he may have arrived at the right place. "Then did he play Looby Loo?" Dwayne persists.

"Perhaps he did. Dwayne, your car is at it again. Maybe you need to make a garage. Your car is looking for a home."

Dwayne squints at me and smiles. "My car is

lookin' for that Magpie guy," he says, sitting down next to me at the table. He pulls over the Lego container and begins to surround his car with walls. "This place over here, that's for Magpie."

I know an invitation to play when it comes my way. I cup my hand and pretend Magpie flies into Dwayne's garage. "There. He'll be happy to visit your car for a while. Maybe you could make him a little nest? What do you think?"

🌿 Unavoidably, I am away for several weeks. By the time I return, Alex has a new baby sister and Vassi has told her first story. These, at least, are Thea's two pieces of news when I join her and Allegra at the story table. They are still drawing rainbows.

"I'll do blue first," I say, as if no time has passed. "Then green. I might decide to make my own green by coloring yellow into the blue."

"*We* started with red," Thea tells me. "And Alex's baby is Elissa."

"What was Vassi's story about?" I ask, imagining a story about a little girl whose birthday was spoiled. Apparently such minor annoyances hold no interest for Vassi. Her story is about two sisters who find a microwave in the woods.

"A microwave? Really? That surprises me."

"Why?" Thea wants to know. She seems surprised that I am surprised.

"I guess it's because when I was little there was no such thing as a microwave. I am surprised to hear of one in Vassi's story. But why not? Maybe everyone has one nowadays."

Allegra studies my rainbow and asks for my yellow crayon. "Did Princess Alexandra have a microwave?"

"No, she didn't. That story happened long ago. People used a wood fire for cooking. They made the fire inside an iron stove or in a fireplace."

"But not Magpie, right?" Thea draws a V-shaped bird flying over her rainbow. I copy her winged figure in the lower right hand corner of my paper. Next to it, I make a stick drawing of a kneeling girl with unruly hair. "Beatrix made him a nest of pine needles and moss. Magpie's food didn't need to be cooked since it was mostly seeds and berries."

"Bugs and worms too," says Dwayne, pulling up a chair. He appraises our rainbows, then grabs three crayons and begins his own jagged version. Thea watches his fist moving the crayons across the page but makes no comment. She has something else on her mind. "Do witches get married?" she asks.

"Yeah yeah they do," Dwayne answers. "*Everyone* gets married. My other daddy told me that. Even birds do." He looks at me for confirmation.

"Magpie does, that I'm sure of. He meets Lady Nell and they build their nest in the old oak tree that stands beside Beatrix's cave."

My narrative has jumped to a new place. Magpie, it seems, is about to take on the parental role. He and Beatrix were always able to pull me into unexpected paths, changed from year to year, to suit the meanderings of each new group of kindergartners. But how will I stay a step ahead of my story in a room where I am only an occasional visitor?

Lillian comes in from the twos with a fresh supply of story paper. She sits down and examines the sign-up sheet. "I'm going to tell a rainbow story," Allegra says.

"Let's see, now, you're number three on the list," Lillian replies. "Can you remember your rainbow story until then? It's Mike's turn first. Where are you, Mike?" His name is represented by a large M that takes up three spaces on the story list.

He is nearly hidden inside a fort made of boxes and blocks, and emerges quickly, sticking a cardboard sword into the back of his jeans. Thea and Allegra move their crayons and rainbows closer to the storyteller but Dwayne abandons his picture. Instead he takes a superhero figure out of his pocket and offers it to Mike. "You want to do X-ray Man?"

"Uh-uh," Mike says. "I'm doin' a mountain story."

"Oh yeah, I forgot," Dwayne nods, standing X-ray Man on the table facing Mike. "He's gonna listen to you then, okay?"

"Okay." Mike turns to Lillian. "So there's a mountain," he says as if he's never told the story before. "Rabbit climbed up and up and then he falled. And the dad carries him up the big tall mountain."

"X-ray Man, he could really carry him," Dwayne says.

"Yeah, I know." But Mike's story goes no further, not yet. When will Rabbit scale the mountain by himself? Dwayne and I are not alone in wondering what Mike has in mind. Several children have stopped to listen. What an amazing phenomenon this is: a four-year-old is able to create moments of delicious suspense for us merely by repeating a character's failure to climb a mountain. He has heard of mountains in a parent's story and, from this alone, he manages to convey the frustrations of being small in a world of unreachable goals. Could this be why the girls keep drawing their rainbows, a great object at great height yet amenable to their exacting control?

Mitya drops a checkerboard in front of me. "Play by me, is okay?" he asks. The invitation comes because I am the only unoccupied adult at the moment. I see immediately that Mitya knows how to play. Even with Alex hanging on his arm, he jumps my piece in his third move, then points to a jump I must make. "This is to do," he says politely.

It is Thea's turn to tell a story. Her signature on the list is so tiny I need my glasses to read it. She sits silently for what seems a long time, glancing at me in a way I cannot decipher. Her stillness attracts the attention of everyone at the table.

She takes a deep breath, her eyes on me again. "There was a baby bird," she begins, "and the girl finded him. He fell out of a tree and that girl is a witch."

Lillian flashes me a surprised look. "Magpie and Beatrix," Thea goes on. "That's their name. He's . . ."

96

She leans over and whispers to Allegra who mouths a single word. "Oh, yeah, he's adopted," Thea says.

Mitya looks up from the checkerboard. "Vot is Megpie?" he asks and Lillian bursts out laughing. "I guess Mrs. Paley has been mentioning a bird she is fond of, Mitya. She's told Thea and Allegra about him and . . ."

Dwayne jumps up. "Me too! Magpie knows me too!" he says.

"You mean you know Magpie," Thea corrects him.

"So that means he knows me," Dwayne insists, "'cause he heard me talkin' about him."

Thea is impressed by Dwayne's idea of reciprocity. "Does X-ray Man know me?" she asks, watching Dwayne move the figure back and forth. "If I talk about him, will he know I'm Thea?"

"If you play with him. Then he will. Like if you put him in your story."

The entourage at the table waits for Thea's decision. Lillian says nothing to influence her but readies herself for the next sentence. Instead, Thea requests to have the story read back to her. The drama at the story table supersedes all others as we stare at Thea, Dwayne, and X-ray Man.

Will Thea change the plot to include Dwayne's present symbol of happiness? Dwayne, after all, has not, in the past, gone out of his way to make Thea happy. And yet, she once saved him from sinking in the Moscow River, and furthermore, did he not sit beside her and draw a rainbow?

Dwayne reaches over and places X-ray Man in front of Thea, manipulating him into a sitting posture as if listening to Thea's story. She picks up the figure and examines it closely. "Does he fly?" she asks.

Dwayne nods yes. "He don't even need wings to fly."

"Oh, then, good. Beatrix sees X-ray Man flying by and asks him you want to be adopted too? But he says no thank you because I already have a friend that is Dwayne."

"Shall I write all that down?" Lillian asks.

"It's part of my story," Thea informs her, and Lillian glows with pleasure. These are the events we wait for in a classroom, when one human being reaches out to another in perfect harmony.

"But then Magpie comes," Thea says.

"And then . . .?" Lillian wants Thea to say more.

"That's the end. Magpie comes."

"Good. Now you've got us wondering about Magpie," Lillian laughs. "Let's get Mrs. Paley to tell us more."

🍃 "Lady Nell had something important on her mind. Magpie could see that. She hardly seemed to notice him when he returned to the nest with a piece of birthday cake from Princess Alexandra's party. 'Sh-sh-sh,' she whispered. 'Come take a look, Magpie.'"

It is almost going-home time. We have gathered on the rug for my first official Magpie story. Thea has already launched two of the major characters in her own story and told everyone about the disappearing cake during afternoon snack. She has even given me a gentle push in the direction she would like to see me go by asking, "Then, after the birthday party, what did Magpie do?"

Looking past the children on the rug, I see Alex snuggling in Lillian's lap, a sad little boy chewing on his yellow blanket. He worries these days about his mother, at home with the new baby. It is not an easy time for a two-year-old about to turn three.

His preoccupation with babies enters my story.

"'Sh-sh-sh, careful, Magpie. Peek under me and you'll see a lovely sight.' Lady Nell lifted her wing and Magpie gasped, 'Of all things!' Then he counted, 'One, two, three, four, five. Five beautiful eggs!'

"Lady Nell counted them again herself. 'One, two, three, four, five,' she murmured, as if she could hardly believe all these eggs were theirs. 'Don't you love the color, Magpie dear? Grayish white with bits of yellow.'

"She was mindful not to move about too much, though she knew the eggs must be turned from time to time. 'We'll have to sit on them oh so gently and keep them warm.'

"'*We* sit on them?' Magpie hadn't realized that fathers are also egg sitters. 'If you'd prefer to do all the sitting, my dear, I'll be happy to bring home the food we need.'

"'Thank you, Magpie, but it is simply not done that way. It's true that it was up to me to lay the eggs but, in everything else concerning our babies, we must take turns.'"

Alex frowns in my direction and drops his blanket. The change in his demeanor does not go unnoticed. Allegra retrieves his blanket for him and remains at Lillian's side, leaning against her and holding on to the ribboned edge of the blanket.

"Magpie touched each egg with a wing feather. 'Lady Nell, may we invite the children in Schoolmistress's classroom to come see our eggs?' he asked.

"'Of course,' she replied. 'But will they be very quiet and not touch the eggs?'"

I cradle the pretend eggs in my hands. "Let's show Lady Nell how quietly we can tippy-toe past the nest, shall we? Come Annabella, come Alexandra, and Raymond, everyone come see the eggs. Lady Nell is lifting her wing so we can peek in."

Without further instructions, the olders file past me. Thea counts, "One, two, three, four, five" as she stares into my cupped hands and the others do the same. Alex, however, is clearly unhappy with what he sees. He slips off Lillian's lap and begins crawling in our direction. Suddenly he jumps up in front of me and knocks the "nest" out of my hands.

"No babies!" he shouts, bursting into tears. "No babies babies babies!" He runs back to Lillian and throws himself into her arms. Feeling her embrace he stops crying and closes his eyes.

The children study the floor as if real eggs lie broken at my feet, then solemnly return to their positions on the rug, darting worried glances at Alex. He has become part of my story.

"But someone did not want to see Lady Nell's

eggs," I continue. "Raymond sat beside the old oak tree and bowed his head low. Something was making him sad. Magpie flew to his side, brushing his face with a soft feather.

"'It's okay, Raymond. We'll come to see the eggs at another time, just you and me, when it's not so crowded. Or, maybe we'll wait until they hatch.' Raymond looked at Magpie and nodded his head. He knew that the big black-and-white bird was his friend."

"They're keeping Alex home," Lillian tells me when I return the following week. "With the baby and all, Alex can't get himself settled. He's crying too much, nothing they do seems to satisfy him. It's probably for the best, you know." Her voice is cheerful but her eyes are sad. "The thing is, when Maddie returns to work, they'll need a place that takes infants so the children can be together."

Parenting is not as easy for Mrs. Parish as it would seem to be for the deer family I watched this past week in the woods we travel to when we want to escape the city. A mother deer and her two spotted fawns came to our salt block each morning, nibbling leaves along the way. Every few minutes, the doe stopped to nuzzle and lick her babies, and I thought of Alex and his mother reading together in the overstuffed chair next to the school window. In matters of separation and childcare, Mother Deer has fewer decisions to make.

"It's hard to believe that Alex is gone," I tell Lillian. "I keep expecting to see him following Mitya around, meowing and hanging on to him. Now there's no one to call him Moscow. Funny to think of that."

"I feel the same way," Lillian says, "but actually I was the one who suggested that Alex stay home for a while. Two is pretty young to be away when there's a new baby at home. Golly, we miss him though. The twos are going around in circles looking for him."

To the visitor, the children might appear to have forgotten Alex. Simone is still pushing her doll along in the stroller, telling everyone, "Don't wake the baby," while Lamar hammers a mallet into every loose object he can find. Emily, at the play-dough bench, studies Sidney's attempts to roll his car over a pillow, and Valerie curls up in Connie's lap with *The Runaway Bunny*. However, when Stuart sits down at the table Angela is covering with soap suds, she is quick to invoke Alex's name. "That's Alex's chair!" she scolds.

"Oh yeah," Stuart agrees, jumping up. The chair looks the same as all the others but the children know which chair Alex sits on. Stuart runs to the bookshelf and, after a lengthy search, uncovers the old battered copy of *The Little Red Hen*, deliberately avoiding the new edition next to it. He brings the book to Lillian. "By myself," he says, as she turns to the first page.

Stuart has begun to repeat some of Alex's other behaviors too. He follows Lillian into the olders' room and sits on her lap whenever he can. This may have something to do with the fact that his mother is also expecting a baby.

The next day I return to pick up a sweater I left in Lillian's closet and find Mrs. Parish, Alex, and the new baby in their car in the parking lot. It is clear that something is wrong. Alex, still in his car seat, is shaking his head and crying while his mother attempts to calm him.

"Can I be of help?" I ask through the open window. My sudden appearance startles Alex and he stops crying, then he begins again even more loudly, as if to drown out my voice. "Shall I bring Mrs.

Tully?" I suggest, but it is not necessary. Lillian has seen us from the window and is walking toward the car.

"Alex, honey," she says. "Come say hello to Mitya. Look, he's up there in the window waving to you." Alex covers his face with his blanket and turns away.

Mrs. Parish forces a smile. "We'd better leave. This wasn't a good idea."

"I'm sorry, Maddie. Call me tonight, will you? Bye, Alex. I'll come visit you real soon, okay?"

On the way upstairs Lillian makes a sudden request. "Could you manage to come tomorrow, for a few hours at most? It's too late to find a substitute for that short a time. Do you mind, Vivian? I hate to impose, but I can't let Alex feel this way about us."

"I'll be glad to come. Your visit will make a big difference, I think."

"I feel pretty guilty about all of this, you know. It was all too abrupt for Alex. And I did nothing to help. I mean, we sort of *abandoned* him, didn't we? All of a sudden we're gone from his life."

Connie and Maureen are with the twos when I arrive the next morning. "Lillian asked me to come," I explain, knowing they expect me. But I feel awkward.

"Just in the nick," Connie laughs. "Angela is terribly out of sorts. Could you rock her a while, maybe read her a book? She likes *Goodnight Moon.*"

Luckily, Stuart's mother has decided to stay for the morning, influenced perhaps by the realization that Lillian will be gone for a few hours. Or she might simply wish to spend more time with Stuart as she enters the final month of her pregnancy.

Stuart is pleased to have his mother as his companion and occupies her lap at snack time. "My mommy is Lucille," he tells Angela, but when she squeezes her chair in next to them he reacts with annoyance and attempts to push her away. "My mommy," he says, and his mother whispers something to him. "Okay, Mommy, that one," he agrees.

"Stuart wants me to tell his friends about Baby Giraffe at the Lincoln Park Zoo. You know the zoo, you've been there with Mrs. Tully and Connie and Maureen, remember? Well, when I was little we lived just a few blocks from the zoo. We went there every Saturday and the animal I wanted to see was Baby Long Neck, that's what we called the little giraffe."

Stuart stretches his neck and pushes out his chin and a few others copy him. Angela takes advantage of Stuart's new role to reattach herself to his mother and this time Stuart does not object. "Now this little guy kept trying to reach the tall branches where his mom nibbled on the leaves, way up high. He just kept on stretching his neck but that branch up there was too far away. I kept asking, 'When will he be bigger?' and my daddy kept telling me, 'Just wait, you'll see.' But next time and next time Baby Long Neck still couldn't reach. That made me real sad."

"Did you cry?" Angela asks.

"No, but my face looked like this." The children mimic her frown until she switches to a big smile. "Then one day, guess what happened? Someone planted a little tree in the giraffe yard, just big enough for Baby Giraffe to nibble on the leaves, the same way his mom and dad were doing up there on the tall tree. I clapped my hands and laughed."

We do exactly that, clap our hands and laugh. At this very moment Lillian walks in, holding Alex's hand. Valerie runs to him and gives him a push. "By myself!" she shouts, grabbing his hand and pulling him to the table. "Alex's chair, by myself!"

The other twos react with equal purposefulness. Stuart brings *The Little Red Hen* to his mother and says, "Alex's book," and Emily tells Alex that the cat won't help. Nothing has changed, they are saying. You still belong to us and we to you.

"Alex wants a cookie," Angela informs Stuart's

mother. "Baby Giraffe wants a cookie." The connection between the little giraffe's successful reach and Alex's return seems clear to everyone.

🌿 On my way out I hear the familiar sounds of a bad-guy drama in progress and am filled with nostalgia. "Bad guys! We're getting into your house!" "No you're not! We've got iron windows!" The noisy dialogue is coming from the olders' doll corner and I decide to investigate.

In my first decade of teaching I usually took these bad-guy fantasies at face value and called a halt to them as soon as they started. Later, as my curiosity increased, I came to understand that most bad-guy scenarios involved characters in search of a plot and that the plot itself seemed a search for rules to play by. Furthermore, when the play was allowed to continue long enough, the children were usually able to rein in the antiheroes and keep the story going.

It required a move to the preschool on my part for some of these realities to emerge. Kindergarten children were often so well established in their self-stereotyping roles it was not easy to read through the disguises. The threes and fours were newer at the game and therefore I could learn along with them.

Fredrick had been a good one to watch, he of the one-word stories. Being older than Alex, he quickly graduated to monsters, robbers, and other bad guys. He was soon to discover that the older children, the girls in particular, had certain expectations for bad guys who intruded into the doll corner.

When Fredrick told Mollie he was a robber, for example, the older girls reacted confidently. "Don't let him come to your birthday, Mollie," said Libby, who was almost five. "He's just a robber."

"Yeah, I am a robber," Fredrick acknowledged, whereupon Libby, the Thea of the group, countered, "Well, too bad for you, because robbers can't come in the doll corner."

"He can be the father," Samantha decided, helping Fredrick into a vest. Bad-guy conflicts were often resolved by the expediency of changing disguises. Even when the teacher's help was required, it was usually only a matter of altering the fantasy. Which is to say, the offending story was replaced by a more acceptable one.

A year later, Fredrick himself would begin to invent the rules governing bad guys. His first such pronouncement was that bad guys don't have birthdays; they don't have names so they can't have birthdays. "But you called him Skeletor," I reminded him.

"That's his pretend name," Fredrick explained.

Twenty years later in Mrs. Tully's room I am about to hear another version of the relationship between bad guys and birthdays. Such is the timeless nature of doll-corner play.

Entering the room I see that Lillian has turned her back to the conflict; she is concentrating on a checker game between Mitya and Dwayne. But I can tell she is listening to the eruption in the doll corner.

"Give us all your food and money!" Samson and Mike yell, knocking over one of Thea's birthday cakes.

"This isn't food," Thea replies evenly. "It's fairy queen cupcakes. And you can't come."

"Why not?" Samson demands.

"Because bad guys can't have candles." Thea says. "And you can't have princess icing." She sticks pieces of straw into the mold at Vassi's place and asks, "How old are you?"

"I'm a baby just borned," Vassi replies. "I get one candle."

"I'm ten," Mike says sitting down at the table. "I'm a bad guy that's twelve, I mean. That's how old we are." He picks up the damaged cake from the floor and attempts to smooth it.

"La-de-la," Thea tells him, "bad guys can't be how old you are."

"Why not? No fair!"

"Because they can't have candles."

"Why not?"

"Because they don't have a age. And they can't be babies. First you have to be a baby, then you say how old you are."

There is no arguing with her logic. "You could be a hunter," she offers. "Or a prince."

"We're superhunters," Mike says, and Samson adds, "They're good guys."

"Okay, superhunters. Here's ten candles." Thea counts them out, then sticks in four more. "Now you are the oldest. Superhunters are always the oldest."

The doll corner is at peace again. A believable story has been told and, for the time being, everyone has a satisfying role to play.

In Mrs. Tully's Room

The scenes change quickly. Before I can know the outcome of Alex's triumphal return or of the superhunters' uneasy future in the doll corner, I whisk myself away to an Arizona public school. I have come to demonstrate the storytelling and acting that Lillian and I find so engrossing but, as always under these circumstances, I am flooded with doubt. How can I, in so brief an encounter, describe the effects of this kind of theater on a classroom?

The sun is hot as I head out before breakfast to a park near the hotel. Fast walking has become a fairly good substitute for the three-mile run I once relied on to clear my head before a workshop or talk. Today I am in need of clear thinking. The plane trip has left me feeling disconnected and dull and I am certain the schedule is overcrowded.

There will be two classroom visits, one to a kindergarten and another to a class that combines first- and second-grade children. To make time for the teacher sessions that follow, each classroom demonstration is to last only 45 minutes. After the leisurely pace I've become used to in Lillian's room, it seems impossible to accomplish everything in so short a time. The *talking* about storytelling and acting will cut into the time needed for *doing* it.

What if there had been no time for every child to take a turn in Alex's Mama story? Just the thought of that sweet experience makes me laugh and I am instantly in a better mood, remembering my first visit to Lillian Tully's roomful of twos.

A purple finch flies by and settles for a moment in a nearby orange tree. "Such a long way to come," I complain to the tiny bird, "only to have to rush through everything."

The finch darts from branch to branch, fluttering its delicate wings as it pokes into one orange after another. "That's all we'll have time for, you know, just a dab into each story." The purple finch whistles four notes in my direction, which I take to mean, "Don't worry, it will all work out."

The last time I spoke to a bird was in a public square in Canada where I first made the acquaintance of Magpie. I hurry on, past more orange trees, oleander bushes, clumps of prickly pear and saguaro, all waiting for my story to begin. "Once upon a time there was a fussy king who sent his favorite purple finch to find the perfect orange," I say out loud in the deserted park. At this early hour no one is around to wonder why a gray-haired lady is talking to the cactus.

Up ahead an assortment of ducks and geese crowd

together at one end of a pond like children bunching up in the same playground space. "Spread out, why don't you?" I want to shout. "You've got the whole world to swim in!"

A large white heron stands alone on the other side of the pond. Seeing me approach it slowly reenters the water, gazing upward in regal splendor. "Excuse me, Your Highness, have you seen my friend, Purple Finch? He is searching for the perfect orange."

As I draw closer, the elegant creature rises gracefully from the water and settles on a nearby log, emitting a single incongruous squawk in its brief flight. The ducks and geese, as if on signal, begin to swim toward the heron, moving in a circular pattern around the log.

"Quickly, children, find your places, we've no time to lose," the heron orders. "I have a story for you. There was once a purple finch who flew from tree to tree trying to find the sweetest orange for the king's breakfast." I feel myself in rhythm with the heron and its feathery students. My fantasies have prepared me for the day ahead.

Returning to the hotel, I think of a way out of the scheduling dilemma, one that could save at least fifteen minutes. If the children and I begin the activity on the rug and remain there throughout, we will avoid all the delays involved in moving back and forth between table and rug.

But what of those moments of intimacy between child and teacher at the story table? Could Allegra have told her "no one noticed" story in front of the entire group? Would Thea have been so quick to see a connection between Allegra and the girl in the book? Don't we give up too much in the interest of saving time? Yet the need to save time is the reality most teachers face.

I continue to debate these issues with myself through breakfast and almost to the schoolhouse door. The moment I enter the kindergarten, however, my confidence returns. These are the children I know, not different from those in Lillian's school or in my own classrooms. They will rise to the occasion. The need to place a particular image into story form does not depend upon only one special way of doing stories. Furthermore, the pleasure of having one's story acted out will overcome shyness, language obstacles, immaturity, and discontent. In fact the presence of these problems often makes it all the more urgent to tell one's story within a structure that promises the respectful attention of everyone.

Buoying myself with such notions as these, of the sort Lillian and I frequently ponder, I gaze at the mountain range visible through the kindergarten windows. The sun's rays change the mountain peaks from pink to purple much as Thea and Allegra blend the colors of their rainbow, and I can almost see Mike's rabbit valiantly trying to make its ascent. Whatever doubts I have left vanish. It is time to bring on the stories.

"A boy named Mike told a mountain story," I say.

"We have a Mike too!" the children tell me, pointing to a Native American boy.

"Hi, Mike. You'll want to hear this story by another Mike. And when I'm done, you can help us act it out. 'Once there was a rabbit who didn't know what a mountain is. So he went to find one. But when he got there it was so high he fell down. He went up up up again and he fell down again. Then a big tall man who was his daddy carried him up.'"

I show the children the paper I've been reading from, a hastily printed version of the original story. "I'll be happy to write down a story any of you tell me too but first we'll act out Mike's story. Someone can be the rabbit, someone can be the dad, and the rest of us will lift our arms high to be the mountain."

As we lower our arms, several shoot up again, waving in my direction. Oddly enough, there are no mountain stories forthcoming from these children who see them at every turn. Instead, they tell of friends who play in the park and go to carnivals. A candy seller enters the second story, then makes an appearance in those that follow. It is clear that when the entire group listens to each story as it is told, a great amount of copying will result.

Someone is bound to bring the matter up later, I think, glancing at the teachers seated in their chairs against the wall. Perhaps I'll tell them what Lillian would say, that this is the way community begins and friendships are strengthened. My next thought makes me smile: why do I like to quote Lillian so much?

I have a sudden need to tell a story of my own and I give in to the urge. "I saw a white heron early this morning. It sat on a log in the middle of a pond and gave a loud squawk. Then an interesting thing happened. All the ducks and geese swam toward the heron and formed a circle around the log. They looked the way we look, as if the heron was telling them a story and they were getting ready to act it out."

A girl named Maria raises her hand. "Can I tell

one? It's about a little girl and she had a loose tooth. And she had a mom and dad. And her tooth fell out. And the tooth fairy came."

Surprising no one, the next three stories are about loose teeth. "A little girl had lots of loose teeth," says the final storyteller, "so she nailed them all out and got new ones."

"Nailed them out?" I ask.

She nods. "With a hammer."

This eager tooth dismantler, I am told later, is a shy child who rarely speaks in class. When I assure the teachers that this will happen when stories are acted out, they seem doubtful. "You'll discover these things for yourselves," I say. "Everything in a classroom is *local,* as you all know. It's the same with classroom theater. If you do the stories, you'll all do them in different ways and make different discoveries. But one of the things you'll find out is how strong the motivation becomes to tell a story when a child knows it is to be acted out."

"In that case," an observer comments with a grin, "I suggest you prepare yourself for the next group of first and second graders. I think Julia will agree that they may present you with some problems." No one laughs louder than Julia, their teacher. "Tell me about it," she says.

Again, I want to quote Lillian, though more accurately it is Lillian quoting her grandfather. "Funny thing about telling a story, you never know how it'll bounce off somebody. But it'll bounce all right, and it'll land somewhere in its own good time. So don't worry if they don't get it on the first bounce. It'll come back."

As predicted the older children balk from the start. I use one of the kindergarten stories as my demonstration, but the children seem wary of making a commitment. Having been warned of their possible resistance, perhaps I am trying too hard—just the opposite of Lillian and the Mama story which I decide to tell.

"A two-year-old named Alex had a one-word story," I say. "Can you imagine a one-word story? It was 'Mama.' That was his whole story. 'Mama.'" The children smile at each other, a sense of recognition rippling around the rug.

"But here's the part that surprised me. Every other two-year-old wanted to get out there, in the middle of the rug, and act out 'Mama.' They all wanted a turn to be Mama." Every time I say "Mama" a softening and mellowing effect seems to be taking place.

It is the girls who raise their hands, ready to tell a story.

"Once there was a little girl and she wanted a kitty. So she went to the pet store and got a kitty. Then she went outside to play with it." Anna has given us a reliable doll-corner fantasy, one step removed from a Mama story, and the other girls are eager to follow suit. They do not consider the plot too babyish.

One after another, we are told of girls and their pets or of pets looking for owners who, of course, turn out to be lonely little girls. The boys agree to act the animal roles or the pet store owners, but offer no stories of their own. The quick flow of girls' stories may have put a feminine stamp on the activity.

Had the storytelling taken place at a table, away from immediate group scrutiny, it would not have happened this way. When children "do" stories every day, the boys are the most enthusiastic participants. They have the most to gain in being able to put their dramatic images into a more formal presentation; it is their play that is most often discouraged as being too noisy or aggressive.

Nonetheless, here I sit with fifteen minutes left and no hands in the air. I decide to switch to a discussion of play itself. What happens, I ask, when certain classmates are excluded from play? I tell the group about the rule established in my kindergarten, "You can't say you can't play," and there is an immediate response from the boys.

"This certain kid," Jeremy begins ominously, "whenever he came up, other certain people, even girls I think, called him names and made him go away." Seldom have I gotten so quickly to the nub of an unfinished story with a group of children unknown to me. What happened to "this certain kid" is obviously a tale waiting to be continued, though the children are careful not to reveal the victim's identity.

"He called names too," someone suggests.

"Uh-uh," Jeremy states with finality. "No way. He just cried and the teachers told us not to be mean. I mean they told certain people."

Julia smiles at her children encouragingly but, for now, the story seems over. It is time for the children to line up for gym and for the grownups to move to another room for coffee and conversation.

"I see your point," a teacher says when we are settled. "About not knowing what will happen. First, the girls tell all these goody-goody stories, then the boys go off in the opposite direction. Of course, it wasn't a story, it was a discussion." She turns to Julia. "Have you been going over that time on the playground?"

"No, not since it happened. But I agree with you, Fredda. It was so totally different from the girls' stories. This was like, 'Once there was a boy who went to the pet store and told the kitties, "I don't want you!"' There's not a single kid who'd write down such a story but we see the behavior on the playground a lot."

"Let's face it," another teacher says. "We all thought the matter was settled. Obviously it wasn't. Look how guilty everyone feels. No one could even mention Jed's name."

The subject is no longer storytelling and acting. Another sort of narrative has been uncovered but no one is prepared to carry it further, neither the teachers nor the children.

🌿 The next day my schedule is repeated in the same classrooms. After only one day, the new way of doing stories seems completely natural to me; so much for the rigidity of old patterns. Once again the kindergartners need no prompting to tell their stories to which they now add a few complications. There is, in one, a little brother who is refused permission to buy candy and, in another, a family trip that is temporarily halted by a flat tire. There is a lost toy and a bleeding knee, but in all instances, problems are resolved in the next sentence. The brother is given candy by his sister, the tire is repaired, the lost item is found, and the knee is bandaged. For me, the most interesting aspect of the stories today is that each one involves more and more actors until, finally, Jennie has a birthday party and everyone crowds together on stage.

Later the kindergarten teacher summarizes the session. "It caught on—to include more classmates. You know how sometimes a kid will look around and realize some activity he's started has brought everyone in? It's a great feeling and it usually leaves us wondering how did it happen? Look at Jennie, for example. She seldom wants to play with more than one friend. Here she is doing a story that purposely includes the whole bunch. So what's going on?"

"What's going on is *control*," a third-grade teacher decides. "You can let these easy, open feelings come out, you know, let down your defenses, because, in this activity there are external controls that equally apply to everyone. And no one is likely to cut you down for your efforts."

"So it's like pretend pretend?" the principal asks. "You can become your real self in a story, the person you'd like to be, and when it's acted out you can say you're only pretending."

It will not be necessary to quote Lillian any more; these Arizona colleagues are quotable in their own right.

There is a sense of heightened expectation as we enter the first- and second-grade classroom. A small blond boy jumps up when he sees me and begins to speak before anyone else can be called on. "There was this boy!" he calls out. "And this boy wanted a friend. Only no one wanted to be his friend. But then there was another boy that didn't have a friend. So then *they* became friends and they played all day by theirself."

"Is that boy you, Jed?" Serena asks. Her voice is warm and sympathetic, but Jed turns away. "No, it's not me. It's another boy somewhere else."

The group is silent, watching me write Jed's words

on my pad. Then, half a dozen hands go up. "I was first," Juan says. "Can I go?" I nod and he begins.

"There's this boy and he didn't have any friends." A serious connection is about to be made. It is happening right here on the rug, where everyone hears everything at the same time, and it feels as intimate as Thea's response to the "no one noticed" story.

"And this boy he builds himself a big old robot with Legos. And then a monster comes and they fight. And they fight some more and the robot wins. Then everybody likes the robot and they like the boy because it's his robot that he built and they can't see how he did it. So he showed them how. And they are friends."

Later, the teachers and I will agree that these are the magical moments in a classroom when everyone floats together on the same cloud. Nor are the children in doubt as to what has just occurred. One classmate has revealed his pain and another has risen to comfort him. The children know and we know that this is what we are supposed to be doing in a classroom, but sometimes it must be explained in a story before we can see what it looks like. By long wandering a short way has been found.

🍂 Lillian is late on the day I return. "Where was you, Mrs. Tully!" Mike demands, running to greet her on the stairs. "We had our lunch and I did a story and it had a helicopter!"

"I'm sorry, Mike, but I had to see the dentist." She opens her mouth to show him an empty space. "He pulled out a tooth that was hurting me. Too bad I missed your helicopter."

"Rabbit gets into it."

"And goes over the mountain?"

Mike shakes his head. "He can't tell where the mountain's at. Can I see your hole again?"

"Poor Rabbit," Lillian says. "But one of these days . . ."

"He'll climb the mountain." It is Vassi who completes the thought.

I've been away only a week and the world inside Mrs. Tully's room seems altered in significant ways. Rabbit is trying new ways to solve his problem and Vassi has scaled her own mountain.

And so it was in the Arizona classrooms. In only two days the children had begun to reveal something of themselves and their community to me. Yet I am destined to be a collector of unfinished dreams and dramas. What will happen to Jed? I don't even know if he is a first or second grader but this fact seems unimportant. Will Juan's robot story take hold and fly? This is what I would most like to know. I cannot separate Jed from the boy in the story who builds a robot and defeats the monster.

"You didn't show me your hole, Mrs. Tully," Jordan says, fingering a space in his own mouth. "Will it come a new tooth?"

"Yours will, honey, but not mine. I'm too old to grow a new tooth. But the dentist knows how to make one, good as new."

Several other children surround Lillian, wanting to look into her mouth but appearing anxious at the same time. "This reminds me of Grandpa's big toothache. Oh my, didn't he go around moaning and groaning. Grandma told him to go see Dr. Ambrose but Grandpa said he was too busy.

"So he just kept complaining instead. Ohh! And ahh! And the animals in the barn copied him, 'moo-ahh' from Miranda and 'grunt-grunt' from Ellie the pig. Grandma's yellow canary sang out of tune and sweet Bella the goldfish went into hiding. Finally Grandpa said, 'Okay, okay, I'm going to see Dr. Ambrose right now!' Which he did. And when he came back, wasn't he smiling. 'Don't know why everyone made such a fuss. I'm going to get me a nice new tooth.'"

On request, Lillian shows Jordan her empty space again and asks to see his. There are fewer loose teeth in preschool than in kindergarten or first grade. Jordan, Thea, and Mitya have lost one each and Thea's permanent tooth is halfway up.

"You might could get a tooth from the tooth fairy," Thea tells Lillian, then turns to me to ask if I know the tooth fairy.

"I've heard lots of stories about her," I say. "In fact, just last week some kindergarten children had a tooth fairy story for us to act out."

"Can you tell it to me?" Thea urges.

I flip open the pages of my notebook, the same one I used in Arizona. "Here it is. 'Once there was a little girl and her tooth was very loose. And she had a mom and a dad. And her tooth fell out and the tooth fairy came.'"

Thea examines my notebook, as if realizing for the first time what I write in it. "Is my story in here?" she asks.

"I've got a few of yours, Thea." I am about to find them when she asks me another question. "Did you tell those other kids about Magpie?"

"There wasn't time for that. But maybe there will be today. Mrs. Tully asked me to save my story for the end of the day. Then everyone can hear about Magpie and Lady Nell."

"Can you tell me just one thing?"

"I haven't figured out the story, Thea. But I'm pretty sure the eggs haven't hatched yet." I notice Allegra, stretched out on the floor drawing a picture on a huge piece of newsprint. "There might be another sort of surprise for Lady Nell and Magpie. By the end of today, the whole story will come into my mind."

"Are you making it up?"

"Yes, I'm making it up, just the way you do."

"Magpie's not real?"

"No. But in my mind he is."

"Oh."

When the last block has been restored to its place on the shelf and every scrap of paper is recycled in a corner basket, we gather on the rug. "Now, let me remember where I left off," I begin, but the children are quick to tell me.

"Five eggs . . .

"With brown spots . . .

"In the nest."

"Yes, Schoolmistress brought the children to see

the five eggs in the nest. Just then who should come walking along, very slowly, holding something delicate in her hands? It was Beatrix, Magpie's friend."

"A witch," Dwayne reminds everyone.

"Yes, a witch. Magpie wondered why she walked so slowly. Beatrix almost always ran everywhere she went. She must be carrying something of great value, he thought.

"'Magpie! Lady Nell! Look what I found!' Beatrix called. 'I'm pretty sure it's a purple finch's egg. I searched everywhere for the nest but I couldn't find it. The storm last night must have knocked it loose.'

"Magpie and Lady Nell stare at the egg in Beatrix's hand. It is much smaller than a magpie egg. 'Would you like to put it in with ours?' Lady Nell suggests. 'We could keep it warm.'

"Beatrix smiled. 'I was hoping you would do that.'

"Lady Nell lifted her wing. 'Put the egg here, Beatrix. We'll adopt the little purple finch the way you adopted Magpie.' Lady Nell carefully moved one of her eggs to make room for the new egg. 'Here's a lovely spot for him.'"

"Or her," Thea says.

"Yes, or her. Lady Nell doesn't know yet if it's a boy or a girl."

130

"It's a girl," Allegra says. "They want to adopt a girl."

"You might be right, Allegra."

"Is she a yellow canary bird?" Dwayne asks. The newest sibling is in fact a member of the same goldfinch family as is the yellow canary.

"This bird is very much like Mrs. Tully's grandma's yellow canary bird, only it's purple," I tell Dwayne. "Actually I saw a purple finch in Arizona last week. It was reddish purple, the way it looks when Allegra colors blue and red together."

"But Lady Nell has to be a girl, right?" Dwayne is pinning down some important details and imposing a few of his own. "X-ray Man wants to listen," he says, standing the little figure on my knee. "He's a boy. He's a good guy."

Allegra is suddenly at my side. One by one the others surround us and I know again the feeling of being storyteller in a classroom of children. For a brief time we move together along the same path, and every tree, nest, and bird is in harmony with our journey.

"What color is the new egg?" Thea asks.

"Light pink and dark pink," Allegra says quietly and her facts go unchallenged.

🍂 In Mrs. Tully's Room

🍂 At my second evening meeting, several parents greet me by name. They know me as Mrs. Tully's friend, a retired schoolteacher who comes to listen to the children's stories. To my surprise, Alex's mother is there. "Have the eggs hatched yet?" she asks, exploding with laughter when she sees my expression.

"Mitya tells us your stories," she explains. "I've started babysitting him. First he came to play and then we made it official. They need a sitter on weekends when they have to work and I need the money. And, of course, Alex wants his friend Moscow."

It takes a few moments to digest her news but my curiosity is not satisfied. "I'm trying to figure out why you're here," I admit. "Weren't you planning to enroll Alex and his sister in another school?"

"My mother convinced me not to do that," Maddie says. "Elissa is not a calm baby. She needs to be held a lot and played with. We can all see this. No infant program can give this sort of attention. Elissa needs to be with me. So Mrs. Tully had an idea. She's hired me to help with the twos and I can bring Elissa with me. I'll be ready in about two weeks. Meanwhile I'm sitting for Stuart's family too."

"It's a great arrangement," I say. "Mrs. Tully is lucky to have you."

"I'm the lucky one," Maddie replies. "You know Maureen in the twos? She's leaving. Not that she wants to, but she needs more money. Childcare doesn't pay well, but for me, we'll come out ahead. And I'll go back to school when Elissa's older and sleeping through the night. John can be home in the evenings with the kids."

The meeting begins when Bernie arrives. He is the main speaker tonight. After a few announcements, Lillian introduces the discussion. Its title, printed in her newsletter, seems a profound and original statement of her goals: "Preparing Your Child for Fifth Grade."

Lillian will speak first. "Some of you were surprised to see fifth grade mentioned as our subject. You even said to me, aren't we supposed to be preparing for kindergarten? You're worried that your children might not be ready for kindergarten and here I am bringing Bernie in to talk about fifth grade."

Several late arrivals walk in and Lillian waits for them to find chairs. "I must tell you it bothers me a lot that we're all made to worry about kindergarten so much, and first grade too, as far as that goes. It's not your fault, no, it's entirely the school's fault. Well, Bernie has taught all the grades from first to fifth, and he's seen how this has happened over the years, this speeding up of pressure, pushing down into kindergarten."

There is an air of expectation in the audience, perhaps more so than when the topic was punishment. It occurs to me that parents are less certain and more anxious about this issue. Lillian invites people to speak, but when no one responds, she continues.

"Now I'll admit I'm prejudiced in this matter. When *we* were five, my brothers and I were not even in school yet. In our town, school began in first grade, not just for poor kids but for everyone. You stayed at home and played until you were six. And nobody ever worried about us being ready for first grade. This is an entirely new notion, my friends, even here in Chicago. Mrs. Paley also played at home until first grade. Uh, George, you look like you want to say something."

"Yeah, I guess I do." A large man stands and looks at the others. I see from his name tag that he is Stuart's father. "Look, my mother tells us the same thing about Stuart going to kindergarten. Not to worry. She remembers bringing my older sister to school, to first grade in Cleveland, and the teacher was putting the letter 'A' on the board. *In first grade,* showing them the alphabet! But now is now, I tell my mom."

George stops to wipe his face and gulp down a cup of water. "Now is different. Kids are expected to know all their letters and numbers and sounds and plenty of words too before they enter first grade. And if your kid isn't there yet, they blow the whistle on him and start bringing in all those 'special ed' people or what have you." He sits down abruptly but then adds, "So what difference does it make how things used to be?"

Lillian nods solemnly. "I know. George is right. The first-grade teachers expect your kids to come with a writing portfolio and a big jump up on reading." Her face is stern. "Believe me, they'd rather *not* have to teach this way. They know it's wrong to put all that pressure on kids, but they feel trapped by the system. And so we're forced to stop doing what we ought to be doing with young children in preschool and kindergarten."

Another father laughs. "Mrs. Tully, I'd like to meet the person who can force you to do a thing you're not in favor of!" The tension in the room relaxes and Bernie gets up to speak.

"I can see you know my wife," he says, jovially, then proceeds to his main points. "Okay, you've mentioned what worries the first-grade teachers but I'll tell you what fifth-grade teachers talk about. Most children have learned to read and write well enough to be on their own, maybe with some motivation from us, sometimes a little extra help. What worries us more is how *mean* the kids are to each other. They do not play as well together as they did in preschool."

Bernie stops to let his words sink in. Seldom have I seen a group of parents more attentive to the speaker. "Why, sometimes I think the very idea of *together* has faded away and the notion of *separated* has taken its place. The students no longer accept each other as equal partners in work or play the way your kids do. The teachers in my school are seeing these changes as early as first grade and it worries us. We have to ask ourselves, does at least part of this have to do with all this pressure we put on the kids, that maybe we're the ones who start separating them, in mind and spirit?"

All I can think of right now is, what a rousing good speech! If only more teachers would get up at faculty meetings and say these things. Nor is Bernie finished. He continues on the same theme.

"Our fifth graders don't do too well in respecting each other's opinions and stories and in sympathizing with someone else's problems and wanting to help them succeed. So, you know what I tell my colleagues? I talk about my wife's school, how your children learn to listen to each other and try out each other's ideas."

All the while Bernie is speaking, Lillian has not taken her eyes away from his face. It is as if she has never heard him before and doesn't want to miss a word. "I tell my colleagues how Lillian is able to connect friendship to literature, to everything the kids do and learn. And you know what? Several of the teachers have come to watch. Some want to adapt these ideas in their own classrooms, a way of bringing the older children together again, all going in the same direction."

Alex's mother raises her hand. "I'm Maddie Parish," she says. "My Alex is in the twos and I come around pretty often so I've seen all this that Mr. Tully is talking about, how these kids learn to listen to the other guy. And how no one holds it against someone if they're acting in an odd way and all. I watch to see how Mrs. Tully does it and how the kids, even the twos, love coming here and . . ."

She sits down in mid-sentence, her hands trembling. Maddie is not accustomed to public speaking but, in her eagerness to spread the message, she is transformed into a speaker of force and conviction. Nonetheless, she is grateful when the next speaker introduces herself.

"I'm Monique, Shelly's mother. I agree with Maddie but still and all I do worry about the academics. My daughter will start kindergarten in September and she doesn't seem ready, to us. All she wants us to do is play with her and read to her and act out her little stories."

Lillian laughs. "So I guess we've taught her pretty well then? Sorry, Monique, I couldn't help but say that. Go ahead."

"No, you're absolutely right, you have taught her well and she loves school because of these things. That much we can see. But if we try to interest her in something else, nothing doing. Like practicing her numbers and alphabet and sounds, you know. Anyway, we're pretty tired at the end of the day and so is she."

The moment Monique sits down, Darlene, seated next to her, takes up the argument. "The same with us. Dwayne feels totally safe and successful here but he has no interest in these workbooks we buy. He'll color in the pictures and that's it. Probably because we're doing it wrong. At school he wouldn't be so negative about it."

Lillian thanks the speakers for bringing up the subject of workbooks. "I'm not about to belittle your concerns," she says. "You've all heard me say that what we do here are the real academics of the early years: language and sensible thinking and good play and a love of stories. But I do know how anxious you are about the more formal activities, the sort you find in those workbooks you've been buying. It seems more like school."

My impression is that the majority in the room side with Monique and Darlene, but Lillian shows no discomfort. "So let's do some of that, why don't we? How about if we plan a special meeting and you can bring those workbooks to the meeting. No, better yet, bring them to me when you drop off your children and I'll make copies of some sample pages. Then, at our next meeting, we'll do a lesson, the way we might do it at school, and you can offer your ideas. Then we'll all be on the same . . . uh . . ."

"On the same page," Bernie helps her out. It is clear that the parents are relieved. They did not expect Lillian to welcome their workbooks since she uses none in school. I could inform them that Lillian's approach to education is in the best progressive tradition, but her willingness to accept their ideas goes beyond any labeling of method or material. It is from her own tradition of open-mindedness and appreciation of differences that her invitation comes.

Bernie takes the floor again. "One last thing. I want to tell you about the little books your children bring home, the ones made by my fifth graders. This activity has had a great effect on my kids."

Several parents call out their thanks. "That one you made for Rosa, the whole family loves it," a woman says. "Tell that girl Rebekah we want to thank her, will you please? How did she do it?"

Bernie is pleased. "I'll tell you how. First I give my kids a few facts about a child, that Rosa, for example, drags a lady's purse with her wherever she goes and she wears a polka dot hat. Then someone, in this case Rebekah, says she wants to do the book. So I'll give her another fact, that Rosa likes to walk the baby dolls in the little stroller. So Rebekah draws pictures of a little girl in her hat with a big purse and a baby. And she'll put a few words on each page."

Rosa's mother takes the book out of her handbag. "I brought it with me. Listen to this. 'Rosa is the mother. Rosa goes for a walk. Rosa plays with the baby.'" The book is passed around and admired by all. When it reaches Aaron's father, he stands and holds the book high.

"We've got one of these at home, too. A boy named Larry did it, about Aaron and his grandfather's dog, Solo. You can't imagine what this meant to my dad. Tell Larry how grateful we all are, would you?"

I think of Aaron and Samson fighting over the possession of a car. Their spirits were restored by the vision of a peaceful barn where the milk is sweet and baby animals do not feel threatened. Were Lillian to describe that event the parents might better understand why she seldom gets around to "B is for ball."

Yet, in subtle ways, Bernie's little books, each one to be read, carried about, and acted out on behalf of an individual child, explain a great deal about what is important in Mrs. Tully's room. That she is now willing to add an occasional workbook page to the narrative will not diminish the personal nature of the world she creates. "B is for ball" can become part of the classroom story without disrupting the drama on the main stage.

Bernie drives me home while Lillian stays to

chat with a few parents. "That was a good meeting," I say.

"You bet. No one makes more sense to the parents than Lillian does. You know why? Because the parents make sense to her. And the kids see this. It's one of the many things that make them feel safe in her school."

"It's interesting, Bernie, how easily Lillian compromises on the workbook issue but not when it came to punishment, at the last meeting."

At the next stoplight, Bernie turns to me. "My wife will never budge on the subject of punishment. She won't give an inch. This is basic to who she is. The workbooks are peripheral. It doesn't matter that much to her. But she will not teach in a classroom and probably not in a school where children are punished for being young and inexperienced. She considers it abuse. Every teacher and parent who works with her has to accept this and get over the hurdle if it's a problem for them."

🌿 I look at the calendar and know it is time to leave Mrs. Tully's room. One visit has extended to many and nearly four months have passed. Prior commitments that seemed so far off are suddenly at hand.

My last day coincides with Maddie Parish's first day on the job. She is assembling Elissa's portable crib and playpen when I enter the room. "Mrs. Tully told us you won't be coming any more," she says.

"I'm going to miss you all. The way Alex did, I guess. Look at him, rounding up his favorite toys and books. Does he still love the little red hen?"

"He's got a new one. *The Little Engine That Could.*"

"I think I can, I think I can . . ."

"Day and night," she laughs, "that's what we hear. We took the Amtrak to North Carolina and my daddy gave Alex this beat-up old copy that used to be mine. Well, that was the last of the little red hen. Everyone in the family had to read him the little engine book."

"What I'm wondering is, did Alex remember to ask about the runaway wagon, the one in your story?"

Maddie smiles at me. "You recall that? Oh, yeah, you write things down, that's why. Well, as soon as we got off the train, even before he gave my dad a hug, Alex said, 'Where's Mama's wagon at?' It was on his mind."

"And he didn't need to write it down." We both laugh and suddenly I know how much I will miss these visits.

A few minutes later, Lillian takes me aside. "I told the children why you can't be with us after today."

"What did you say?"

"That you have to visit other children in other schools and listen to their stories. Thea said, 'She wants to tell them about Magpie.'"

"Thea knows me better than I know myself." I reach into my bag. "I do at least have a parting story for the olders. In fact, I've done what Bernie's class does, made a book." It is a large spiral pad with cardboard covers and heavy white pages, the kind artists use for sketching. On one side of each double page are pictures I have drawn in a style not unlike a child's and on the other side, my story.

At the end of the day, when the children come together for "long-story time," I show them what I have made for them. "It's like the books Mr. Tully's children make for you, but this one is about Magpie and Lady Nell and their babies."

"Who told them the story?" Dwayne asks.

"Do you mean because it's written down? I told the story to myself and printed the words. And now I'll read it to you. It's called 'The Eggs Hatch.' That's what these three words on the cover say."

🌿 Lady Nell heard a tap-tap-tap coming from the purple finch egg. "Listen, Magpie, one of our babies is starting to hatch."

"And it's moving a tiny bit," Magpie said. "Look, the others are doing it too. How long will it take for them to crack their shells and come out? Can we help them?"

"No, Magpie, they must do it for themselves. The tapping and cracking helps them become stronger. It will take them a day and a night. By tomorrow morning, all our babies will be hatched, five magpies and one purple finch."

When Schoolmistress and her children came to the nest, the babies' mouths were already wide open crying to be fed. Magpie and Lady Nell were flying back and forth bringing food to their hungry family but they stopped long enough to introduce each baby to the children.

"This is our first born, Lady Beatrix. The purple

finch is a girl, you see, named after our dear friend Beatrix who found her."

The children began to clap but Magpie reminded them not to frighten the babies. "They're very young, you see. Just one day old."

"Sorry, Magpie," Alexandra said. "We promise to be quiet. Can you tell us all their names, please?"

"Of course. There are three girls and three boys, and you've met Lady Beatrix. This is Lady Olivia and Lady Oriana." Magpie touched each one with his beak as he spoke her name.

Then he named the boys. "This is Ram, this one is Vinnie and, finally, here is Xavier. Now you have met all six."

Raymond wondered if the babies knew their own names yet but he decided Magpie and Lady Nell were too busy for more questions.

"We take turns feeding the babies," Lady Nell explained as she returned to the nest with a beak full of worms and berries.

"And we'll take turns keeping them warm too, until each one is completely dry and fluffy," Magpie added. "Come tomorrow and you'll see how different they look."

On the way back to school, Schoolmistress sang

the names of the new baby birds and the children repeated each one after her.

"Lady Beatrix, tra-la-la."

"Lady Beatrix, tra-la-la."

"Lady Olivia, la-de-da."

"Lady Olivia, la-de-da."

By the time they got to "Xavier, Xavier, dum de dum" the children knew all the names by heart. Lady Beatrix, Lady Olivia, Lady Oriana, Ram, Vinnie, and Xavier. Now there would be six babies to watch and tell stories about. And one day, the little birds would be old enough to tell their own stories.

🌿 I close the covers of the book and the children are quiet. Then Allegra asks, "When will you come back?"

"In May, perhaps, when the tulip bulbs you planted are blooming. I'll come then, maybe even sooner if I can."

🌿 As it happens, I return the following week. Lillian has called to tell me of a new kind of story Alex has for them. "I think you'll be surprised," she says. As with her original invitation, I cannot resist.

What sort of story could Alex tell that would surprise his teacher, after all the stories she has heard? I know he is long past the Mama story, having discovered he can put Mitya and Stuart into his stories. He even tried out X-ray Man but couldn't figure out what to do with him. "X-ray Man," he said, and Lillian dutifully wrote it down. But the next sentence was, "Mitya plays with Alex."

The last story of Alex's that I copied into my journal read: "Mama takes Alex to the zoo. To the zoo. To the zoo." I noted at the time that he seemed to be experimenting with rhythms in his storytelling, a poetrylike quality he achieves by repeating the last line.

The twos do not seem curious about my return, though I had said my good-byes a week earlier. Unavoidably I arrive too late to hear the stories as they are dictated but I am in time to watch them acted out.

Valerie greets me at the door and takes my hand. "We're doing stories," she tells me, reminiscent of my first day in the class. I follow her to the rug and place my chair behind the group.

148

Her story will be first. She has recently turned three and her story sounds more like a three-year-old's. "Valerie and Angela go to the park. And they play. And Mommy lets me play." The two girls walk around the rug, then sit down and pretend to dig. "And dig," Valerie adds. "You have to dig," she tells Angela.

Alex is next. He looks at his mother seated nearby, then curls up in the center of the rug as Lillian reads his story. "The baby is sleeping. Mama is the baby. He brings the bottle."

The children have heard this story of his before. They are not surprised, nor do they seem confused by the fact that there is only one character on the stage. Alex, the baby who is also the mother, puts three fingers in his mouth.

When Valerie's story is acted out, several children want a turn to walk in the park and dig a hole. No one, however, asks to be the mother-baby in Alex's story. Perhaps they understand that it is a private scene, one they cannot share. I am grateful that once again Lillian has allowed me to view the never-ending and always new phenomenon of the young child as storyteller.

Before I leave, I stop in to say hello to the olders

and am greeted with "Where's Magpie?" I apologize for being unable to stay long enough for a Magpie story, explaining that I am on my way to the airport. I even show them my airplane ticket.

"Mrs. Paley stopped by to listen to Alex's story," Lillian says. "I called her on the phone and told her Alex is doing a new kind of story."

"What is it?" Thea asks.

"Here, I'll read it to you," I say. "I copied it into my notebook. 'The baby is sleeping. Mama is the baby. He brings the bottle.'"

"Is that a new kind?" Dwayne asks.

"Well, the mama *is* the baby. And Alex is both at the same time."

No one seems to find this notion strange or new. "That's just the stories Alex likes to tell is all," says Dwayne. "He could be that. I mean he really *is* that."

Lillian and I look at each other. Does Dwayne mean Alex can pretend to be both mother and baby or rather, is he wondering if, in some way, the mother is still part of Alex, not separated from him because there is a new baby? This is something we must write about in our letters. Lillian, of course, is in a far better position to find out what Alex and Dwayne have in mind.

🌿 In May the tulips stand tall in their splashy colors and the gardens remind me of Allegra's rainbows. It is time to visit Mrs. Tully's school again.

"When I was little I thought tulips had to be red," I say to Thea and Allegra. We've been sent to gather lilacs from the bushes that grow along the fence and have stopped to examine the tulips.

Smoothing a patch of dirt with my foot, I scratch out the zigzag shape we always used for tulips. "Up, down, up, down, up, down, three points, color it red and add a green stem. There! A tulip."

The girls borrow my twig and make their own outlines next to mine. Then they name the colors of Lillian's tulips. "Red, white, yellow, pink, orange, purple finch . . ."

"Purple finch? Is that what you call the purple tulip?"

"Mrs. Tully calls it that."

How good to be back in this place where stories are not lost and forgotten. "Did Rabbit climb the mountain?" I ask while I snip lilacs and hand them to the girls.

"Mike doesn't want him to," Thea says. "Sometimes a tiger carries him. Or a lion."

Allegra kneels on the ground and uses her finger

151

to draw another tulip. "But he's not Rabbit now. He's the lion."

"Hmm. I'm not surprised. People do pretend to be other characters." I give Allegra the next sprig of lilacs. "The first time I came to visit, you told a story about a girl nobody noticed."

"Then she noticed a red chair with pink roses," Thea remembers. "I mean, that was in my story."

We gossip on the bench as we separate the flowers into three baskets. "By the way, does Alex still visit the olders in the afternoon, now that his mother and Elissa are here?"

The girls nod. "And we visit Elissa sometimes," Thea says. "Mrs. Parish lets us wheel her in the stroller if we're careful. Very careful."

"The boys are not careful," Allegra shakes her head. "Only Mitya is. He likes going slow."

They learn to know one another so intimately: this is the way someone walks and runs, holds a book, draws a picture, tells a story, likes a certain activity and grows sullen doing something else. If we know these things about each other, they seem to say, we cannot be strangers. And always, it is the play and the stories that produce the most useful information.

"Why doesn't Mike want him to?" Allegra asks Thea.

"Because Rabbit won't be little any more, and Mike rathers to be the lion."

As we bring our baskets into the building I feel giddy with pleasure, anticipating the day ahead. A large bird flies by the staircase window. "What do you think, Magpie? Can I do it?"

"Can you do what, Schoolmistress?"

"Is it possible to spend a lifetime watching the little ones, wondering about everything they say and do?"

"Lady Nell and I often speak of these very same matters," Magpie replies. "Our children are growing so fast they'll soon be on their own. It makes us sad to think about it. But then we remember that in the spring we'll have a new family and each new baby will be a surprise."

Schoolmistress is overjoyed. "Of course! What a lovely thing to remember. All these new children coming along and all the surprises waiting for us. We really are quite fortunate, don't you think?"